NICK ENRIGHT trained for the theatre at New York University School of Arts, where he studied playwriting with Israel Horovitz. His plays include *On the Wallaby, Daylight Saving, Mongrels, A Property of the Clan, Blackrock, Good Works, Chasing the Dragon* and *Spurboard*. With Justin Monjo, Nick adapted Tim Winton's *Cloudstreet* for the stage. With composer Terence Clarke, he wrote the musicals *The Venetian Twins* and *Summer Rain*. Other musicals include *Miracle City* with Max Lambert, *Mary Bryant* with David King, and the book for *The Boy from Oz. Cloudstreet* and *Good Works* won the Melbourne Green Room Award for Best Play, and *Daylight Saving, A Property of the Clan, Blackrock* and *Cloudstreet* all won Australian Writers' Guild AWGIE awards. Nick has also written for film, television and radio. He received the 1999 Sidney Myer Performing Arts Award.

One of Australia's most versatile theatrical practitioners, TERENCE CLARKE is known as a director, composer, pianist, actor, musical director, dramaturg and teacher. He was founding Artistic Director of the Hunter Valley Theatre Company; Associate Director of the National Theatre Company, Perth; Artistic Director of the Australian National Playwrights' Centre; and Head of Directing at NIDA. His musical collaborations for the stage include *Flash Jim Vaux* (with Ron Blair), the award-winning *Variations* and *The Venetian Twins* (both with Nick Enright).

From left: Peter Marshall as Mick, Vince Atkinson as Clarrie and Sandro Colarelli as Red in the 1997 Queensland Theatre Company production in Brisbane. (Photo: Paul Aurisch)

Summer Rain

NICK ENRIGHT
and
TERENCE CLARKE

CURRENCY PRESS, SYDNEY

CURRENCY PLAYS

First published in 2001
by Currency Press Pty Ltd,
PO Box 2287, Strawberry Hills, NSW, 2012, Australia
enquiries@currency.com.au
www.currency.com.au

Reprinted 2015, 2021

NATIONAL LIBRARY OF AUSTRALIA CIP DATA

Enright, Nicholas, 1950-.
Summer rain.
ISBN 0 86819 563 4.
1. Musicals – Australia. 2. Country life – New South Wales – Drama.
3. Australia – Drama. I. Clarke, Terence. II. Title. (Series: Currency plays.)
782.140994

Publication of this title was assisted by the Commonwealth Government through the Australia Council, its arts funding and advisory body.

Set by Dean Nottle
Cover design by Lisa White

Currency Press acknowledges the Traditional Owners of the Country on which we live and work. We pay our respects to all Aboriginal and Torres Strait Islander Elders, past and present.

CONTENTS

for Lynne
with love
TC & NE

INTRODUCTION

When Currency Press asked me to write this foreword and the new *Summer Rain* script arrived at my front door, it was as if a ghost from the past crept gently back into my house. It had been eighteen years since I directed NIDA students in the premiere of Nick Enright and Terry Clarke's bittersweet musical. It was a time before Australia had seen *Cats* or *Les Miserables* or *Phantom of the Opera* or *The Boy from Oz*, all of which changed our perceptions of what was possible in musical theatre; a time of innocence and expectation.

Back then, there was constant speculation within the theatre industry about the mythical 'Great Australian Musical'. When would it appear? Perhaps *Summer Rain* which sought a truly idiomatic form of musical and verbal expression was 'IT'. After all, here was a significant pioneering work striving to create a new kind of musical that spoke with an undeniably Australian voice. And, to be honest, few have succeeded since.

Over those eighteen years I have had further collaborations with Nick Enright whom I came to regard as a great teacher and friend (*Miracle City* and *The Boy from Oz*). And Terry Clarke, who I remember faltering in front of at our first meeting in the NIDA Music room when, in my reverent nervousness, I dropped the entire unstapled script all over the linoleum floor and had to crawl on my hands and knees to pick it up, has become one of my most caring supporters and friends.

I read the 'new' script and discovered how much had changed over the previous two decades through various productions and workshops. It had been simplified, some characters were cut and the sprawling story had been focussed and refined. But the beating heart of the piece was unchanged. There it was, this agonisingly tender exploration of the Australian spirit through those lovingly created characters (and those gorgeous songs) all of whom yearned for a life different from the one they were living. They all seemed to be searching for the healing that only forgiveness can bring and the fulfilment of true love.

I had seen the Sydney Theatre Company production but not the more recent one directed by Robyn Nevin at the Queensland Theatre Company. As I turned the pages, I missed a few old friends—characters that had been created for the seventeen students of the 1983 NIDA graduation class. But I was grateful to be reunited with so many of my old favourites. The charming shyster Harry Slocum; his wife Ruby, a hard-nosed 'trooper' with a heart of gold; and Joy, (now though not originally) their daughter, who has grown up dancing in a tent and craves a home. I re-met those indomitable citizens of Turnaround Creek, the taciturn, unforgiving publican Barry Doyle and his cheeky, budding daughter Cathy who senses that she does not belong (and who was orginally Renie's daughter); Mick with his gammy leg who never took the time to understand the longings of his pretty but unhappy wife Peg and almost loses her to a charmer from the troupe who promises a more sensitive and erotic kind of love than Mick could ever express. There were others who had survived the eighteen years, and some who were amalgams created from those who hadn't.

Re-reading the script took me on a journey back into the charming and achingly lost world of 1945 outback Australia. Here the meeting of two 'tribes'—the sedentary townsfolk and the nomadic showfolk—inevitably brings revelations. When the creek floods after the unexpected summer rain and they are stuck together for a few life-altering days it turns out to be, in the finest sense of the phrase, 'a nine-day wonder'.

Domestic as the piece initially seems, a vast canvas of poetic and universal themes form its artistic backdrop. The uncertainty of postwar Australia is reflected in the characters. Where do we go now? Why doesn't life feel quite right any more? It is a cathartic moment historically for the nation and certainly for the inhabitants of Turna, who have tried to live with their heads in the sand for far too long. The outside world is on its way and with it comes confrontation and challenge at the grass roots level. Change is hard. But necessary.

Perhaps 15-year-old Cathy best represents the Spirit of the Future. Defying her sense of displacement and the conventions that have held the others prisoner for so long, Cathy claims independence and embraces the great adventure of life ahead. Her youthful boldness, honesty and fresh perception carry her to freedom. One hopes the same could be said for postwar Australia.

Turnaround Creek is a sort of Forest of Arden where everyone falls in love with the wrong (or right?) person and in so doing redefines their life. This is no superficial high-kicking, all-tap-dancing spectacular, although the show is not without its high points, its humour and its celebration. But finally *Summer Rain* is an intimate exploration of the lives and longings of the principal characters who might begin worlds apart (and some with hidden secrets) yet still come to acknowledge that their common denominators—their humanity and their vulnerabilities—are what really count.

The show's roots are—like Harry Slocum's troupe—firmly placed in the Australian tent show tradition which dates back to the early twentieth century. Back then Australian audiences found a love of vaudeville and its more sophisticated relative, the musical. The forms were passed on to us through the Fuller and Tivoli Circuits, through J.C. Williamson's and through performers such as Roy (Mo) Rene, George Wallace and Gloria Dawn. Its influence is felt today in the works of Dorothy Hewett, Jack Hibberd, Reg Livermore and Nick Enright. *Summer Rain* grows out of and honours this tradition.

The work is also testimony to the unique collaboration between Clarke and Enright. The haunting melody of 'The Casuarina Tree' so well suits its painfully poetic lyrics. The cheeky pub number whose rollicking tune perfectly matches its drunken patter of 'Hear the One About?'. And the celebratory outburst of both song and lyrics when the heavens open and the townsfolk are out in the street with water splashing on their faces and filling their hats as they sing 'Send 'er Down, Hughie'. Rejuvenation. Rebirth. Hope. These are the qualities Enright and Clarke explore so well together.

As in all great musicals, the songs enable the characters to use poetic imagery and reveal their private thoughts. They transform apparently simple stereotypes into complex and continually surprising figures grappling with universal feelings and confusions. They help each character to move, in his or her own way, towards that most confronting thing of all—the truth about themselves. The lyrical, melodic, musical themes and boisterous tunes give the piece a musical 'wholeness', true to both period and psychology, that carries us through an emotional, intimate and uplifting evening.

Yes, there is a kind of magic in this tender musical and if directors and actors can tap that vein, it is a rewarding work both to play and to watch. I remember standing on stage at the NIDA Parade Theatre on the closing night back in 1983, with Nick and Terry and the cast, taking our bows and looking out through the streamers at the audience on their feet applauding wildly, with a look on their faces we had rarely seen before. The show had tapped into the Australian psyche. There was acknowledgement and pride in the eyes of the punters and thanks for a few common and profound insights shared. They had had a jolly good night's entertainment—and so had we.

Gale Edwards

STAGE HISTORY

Summer Rain was commissioned by NIDA. Elizabeth Butcher and John Clark had been producers of the first Sydney Theatre Company (STC) season at the Opera House in 1979 and, therefore, of Nimrod's contribution to that anthology season, our first musical, *The Venetian Twins*. They liked the piece and admired our second show, *Variations* (Nimrod 1982), and asked us to write a musical to showcase their graduating class of 1983. By happy coincidence, Terry had directed the group in *The Cherry Orchard*, and I was head of the acting course; so we knew well the seventeen actors for whom we would be writing.

It's worth noting, since the show is often seen as a valentine to the old tent shows, that it grew out of some improvisations about a rural community, and found its primary impulse in a newspaper photograph of an Australian farmer, kneeling in a paddock, hat upturned, catching the rain which signalled the breaking of another drought. Then we recalled a television interview with that fine actor Ron Falk in which he likened the Australian performer to 'a cactus in the desert', and read Ronnie Shand's reminiscences (in Wendy Lowenstein's oral history, *Weevils In The Flour*) of the tough times of a song-and-dance-man during the Depression. Suddenly there emerged a story of the meeting of two tribes of battlers, brought together as drought breaks and the rain flows.

John Clark and the students greeted the project with enthusiasm, and we spent the year developing it with the actors, designers and technicians and our director Gale Edwards, then a member of the acting staff.

The show opened in October 1983 at the Parade Theatre. The following cast list includes characters cut from subsequent versions:

TROUPE

HAROLD SLOCUM	Ritchie Singer
RUBY SLOCUM	Karen Vickery

JOY LAROCHE	Julie Haseler
BELLE PARGETER	Lyn Pierse
CECIL PARGETER	Dean Carey
GENE DANIELS	Todd Boyce
ILONA	Helen Buday

The rest of the company played the defectors in the first scene (TEXAS, BRYCE, CORA, DIAMANTINA, etc.)

TOWN

BARRY DOYLE	Greg Stone
RENIE MCKENNA/ROSIE	Fiona Press
PEG HARTIGAN	Merridy Eastman
MICK HARTIGAN	Paul Keane
CLARRIE NUGENT	Greg Saunders
CATHY MCKENNA	Tracey Higginson
BETH TOWNSEND	Annie Murtagh
SMACKER HAYES	Dean Nottle
PETER BANNISTER	Steven Vidler
JAMIE TOWNSEND	Andrew Lloyde

Director, Gale Edwards
Musical Director, Terence Clarke
Designer, John Senczuk
Lighting Designer, Ian McGrath
Choreographer, Keith Bain

The size of the cast may suggest the structural problems of this first version. Most musicals, even epics like *Showboat*, have fewer than a dozen principal characters, and two or at most three concurrent stories. We had eighteen principals (with Fiona Press playing the two McKenna sisters) and enough story to fuel half a dozen shows. Inevitably, despite the strength and charm of its production and performance, the show was judged to be overplotted and diffuse; but there was enough enthusiasm for its premise, as well as its spirit and atmosphere, to earn it some influential supporters.

Several years later, the Australian Bicentennial Authority (ABA) offered us funds to develop and refine the show for a full-scale commercial production in 1988. To that end, Aubrey Mellor conducted a workshop in December 1986 at the Seymour Centre. He and the cast helped us towards further discoveries about the show, and gave a rousing showcase performance at the end of our fortnight together. The show went into further development under the aegis of the AETT, and the directorial guidance of Jon Ewing, but the production was shelved in late 1987.

Some months later Richard Wherrett offered us a production of the new version at the Sydney Theatre Company, where it opened in February 1989:

TROUPE

HAROLD SLOCUM	Peter Carroll
RUBY SLOCUM	Nancye Hayes
JOY SLOCUM	Donna Lee
JOHNNY SLOCUM	David Whitney
TONY	Lorry D'Ercole

TOWN

BARRY DOYLE	Bob Baines
RENIE MCKENNA	Valerie Bader
PEG HARTIGAN	Denise Kirby
LORNA FARRELL	Genevieve Lemon
CATHY DOYLE	Alison Sutherland
MICK HARTIGAN	Greg Stone
CLARRIE NUGENT	Jonathan Biggins
RED FARRELL	Ken Radley
MAISIE TRENGROVE	Joanie Thomas
PADDY MCKENNA	Geoff Newmann

Director, Rodney Fisher
Musical Director, David King
Designer, Roger Kirk
Lighting Designer, Nigel Levings
Choreographer, Ross Coleman

There were three major changes to the story. The new show now opened not with the troupe on Christmas Eve, but in Turnaround Creek on Boxing Day; we met the depleted Slocum troupe only on their arrival. Cathy (Renie's supposed daughter in the NIDA version) became the late Nancy's third daughter, sister to Peg and a new character, Lorna. And we established symmetry with the past by making Peg's nine-day lover not Cecil (a married member of the troupe) but a new character, Harold's son Johnny.

The STC production earned neither critical nor popular success, and since the show needed the resources of a large theatre company, it seemed unlikely that it would ever have another professional showing. Despite productions of this version at WAAPA and UNSW, it seemed destined to fall into the limbo where so many Australian musicals lie.

But Robyn Nevin, who had enjoyed the NIDA production, and had faith in the potential of the show, invited us to develop it anew as the opening production of her term as artistic director of the Queensland Theatre Company (QTC). Terry and I returned to the piece with new hope and energy, fuelled by Robyn's enthusiasm and the wise dramaturgy of Janis Balodis.

Terry had always believed that my decision to cut the tent show prologue and open in the drought-stricken town damaged the tone of the show. He was right, as we saw later; but our musical and dramatic solution in Brisbane was still too grim: the troupe, stranded in western Queensland after losing their tent and goods in a fire on Christmas Eve, wait for a train back to Brisbane. Nonetheless, this production, beautifully directed, designed and acted, at last clarified and simplified the show's story while intensifying its emotional life. Relocated to western Queensland, it was a great popular and artistic success; and it was specially satisfying to see a preview which the company played for an audience of retired variety performers, many of whom had known at first-hand the Slocums' world.

This published version (aside from its opening scene) is essentially the result of the development process initiated by Robyn. Her QTC production opened at the Suncorp Theatre in January 1997:

TROUPE

HAROLD	Bille Brown
RUBY	Geraldine Turner
JOY	Elise Greig
JOHNNY	Anthony Weigh

The rest of the company played the defectors in the first scene.

TOWN

BARRY	Peter Adams
RENIE	Gael Ballantyne
PEG	Genevieve Lemon
LORNA	Rebecca Riggs
CATHY	Melissa McMahon
RED	Sandro Colarelli
MICK	Peter Marshall
CLARRIE	Vince Atkinson
MAISIE	Bev Shean

Director, Robyn Nevin
Musical Director, Sharon Raschke
Designer, Dale Ferguson
Lighting Designer, David Walters
Choreographer, Cheryl Stock

Three years later came the opportunity to make a final revision (though 'final' is a word that has taken on some fluidity for us as writers on this show!) when the WAAPA wanted to schedule a production for their final-year musical theatre students. Terry convinced me that to make Harold a compulsive gambler would gain rather than lose the sympathy of our audience, and we restored the NIDA opening scene, with its tent show razzamatazz. We were able to see the results in Leith Taylor's delightful production, and could then settle on this published version, which represents the show as played in Perth in March 2000, with a couple of small cuts and revisions.

This text comes with our thanks to many colleagues: John Clark and Elizabeth Butcher, who commissioned it and loved it; Margaret Helman who was one of those who prompted the ABA to develop it; Richard Wherrett and Robyn Nevin who remembered it and revived it; Gale Edwards, Aubrey Mellor, Jon Ewing, Rodney Fisher, Janis Balodis, Leith Taylor and the actors, designers and musicians who helped to shape it (especially that first NIDA cast who brought such love to it); David King, who offered much musical advice on the STC production; and the friends who have believed in the piece and encouraged us to keep working on it. It is somehow pleasing that a show in which several characters are given a second chance at life and love should itself have been given so many chances to live and grow!

Nick Enright
May 2001

The cast size for a professional production now stands at thirteen. In this published text we have suggested ways for amateur companies to expand the show for a larger ensemble, who could play the other troupe members. We encourage any company that wants to expand the show by adding to the townspeople, to give each member of the ensemble an identity and a place in Turnaround Creek.

CHARACTERS

TROUPE

HAROLD SLOCUM, proprietor of Slocum's tent show
RUBY SLOCUM, his second wife
JOY SLOCUM, his daughter by his first wife
JOHNNY SLOCUM, her brother

Other troupe members (who may double with the TOWNSPEOPLE)

BRYCE BARCLAY
MAGDA LAZSLO
THE FLYING RINELLIS
CORA and DIAMANTINA, the Price sisters
TEXAS
CECIL, stage manager
(This group of characters could be augmented)

TOWN

BARRY DOYLE, a widower, publican of the Shamrock Hotel
PEG HARTIGAN, his eldest daughter
MICK HARTIGAN, her husband
LORNA FARRELL, Barry's second daughter
RED FARRELL, her husband
CATHY DOYLE, 15, Barry's youngest daughter
CLARRIE NUGENT
MISS MAISIE TRENGROVE

SETTING

The action takes place in the nine days between Christmas Eve 1945, and New Year's Day 1946, in western NSW, chiefly in the town of Turnaround Creek.

From left: Todd Boyce as Gene, Helen Buday as Ilona, Ritchie Singer as Harold, Lyn Pierse as Belle and Julie Haseler as Joy in the 1983 NIDA production in Sydney. (Photo: Peter Holderness)

ACT ONE

SCENE ONE

On and offstage in a small town, Christmas Eve, 1945. HAROLD *shows an empty magic box. Drum-roll.*

HAROLD: Where has she vanished, my lovely daughter? Abracadabra… and here she is!

    He makes JOY *appear. Cymbal-clash.*

JOY: The Abracadabra Man, Harold Slocum!

HAROLD: Sad to say, it's the night that's vanished, friends! But to take us out in style, I give you the Queen of the canvas, Ruby Slocum!

    RUBY *enters.*

RUBY: NOW IT'S TIME TO TAKE OUR LEAVE,

HAROLD: Corporal Johnny Slocum, Pride of the AIF!

    JOHNNY *enters.*

JOHNNY: IT'S GOODNIGHT BUT NOT GOODBYE!

HAROLD: Everybody's cover girl, Miss Joy Slocum!

JOY: HERE WITH YOU ON CHRISTMAS EVE,

HAROLD: All the way from war-torn Europe, Magda Lazslo!

    MAGDA *enters.*

MAGDA: VE HAFF FELD ZE EF'NINK FLY.

HAROLD: The long and the short of it, the Price Sisters!

    CORA *and* DIAMANTINA *enter.*

CORA/DIAMANTINA: AS ACROSS THE STAGE WE WEAVE,

HAROLD: That master of disguise, Mr Bryce Barclay!

    Music. BRYCE *doesn't appear.*

  Mr Bryce Barclay!

Music. BRYCE *doesn't appear.*

… is indisposed…

LEAVING BURRENJUCK WITH A SIGH…

TEXAS *and* THE FLYING RINELLIS *join them.*

ALL: SHOWFOLK NEVER GRIEVE, AND WE WANT TO TELL YOU WHY!

CORA/DIAMANTINA: Why?

ALL: MAYBE YOUR LIFE HAS COME A GUTSER,
 MAYBE YOU'RE FEELING WOEBEGONE?

MAGDA: Oh!

ALL: MAYBE YOUR NERVES ARE ALL IN TATTERS?
 WHAT MATTERS IS, THE SHOW GOES ON.
 COULD BE YOU'RE STUCK WITHOUT A PADDLE
 SOMEWHERE WAY UP THE AMAZON—

THE FLYING RINELLIS: Aargh!

RUBY: COULD BE YOU'RE BROKE?

JOHNNY: OR BLUE?

TEXAS: OR BLOTTO?

HAROLD: OUR MOTTO IS,

ALL: THE SHOW GOES ON, AND ON…
 WE'VE BEEN ON OUR UPPERS
 AND SUNG FOR OUR SUPPERS
 FROM BACK OF BEYOND TO LITTLE LON,
 AND WHAT KEEPS YOU GOING,
 AND GOING AND GOING,
 AND GOING AND GOING TILL YOU'RE GONE?
 THE LIGHT IS ON YOU
 AND THE SHOW GOES ON…

Dance break. CECIL, *the stage manager, finds* BRYCE *in the wings, packing his gear into a trunk.*

CECIL: Bryce! This is pretty bloody unprofessional.

BRYCE: Slocum pushed me to it. I gave him till interval. I told him we're paid in full or no second half.

CECIL: The others went on.

BRYCE: I'm a union man, and the union has given me my orders. I'll ask you one last time. Any chance Harold might cough up?

CECIL: And I'll tell you one last time: you'd be lucky.

BRYCE: Then I'll have to call the whole company out.

CECIL: Stop talking like a shop steward. We're in show business!

BRYCE: And the Abracadabra Man is about to witness the biggest disappearing act in show business.

He goes on packing as the number finishes...

ALL: WE CAME ALONG TO ENTERTAIN YOU,
        YOU CAME FROM HITHER AND FROM YONDER.
        SAYING GOODNIGHT IS SUCH SWEET SORROW,
        TOMORROW, THOUGH,
        THE SHOW GOES ON, AND ON.
        THE SONGS AND THE LAUGHTER
        WILL ECHO ON AFTER
        WE'VE PULLED UP OUR TENT-PEGS AND GONE.
        WE SAY TOODLE-OO NOW, TO YOU AND TO YOU NOW,
        BUT SWEAR WE'LL BE BACK WITH YOU ANON.
        SO WAVE US ALL GOODBYE, THE SHOW GOES ON, AND
            ON, AND ON...
        THE SHOW GOES ON!

Applause. The TROUPE *come off.*

HAROLD: Brycie boy! We don't disappoint our public. We may have had a small family difference, but—

BRYCE: I'm not your family, Harold. And there's one big difference between us. You own the show. We do it. And the union says we get paid in full or we walk.

HAROLD: Paid in full? That might be tricky this week.

TEXAS: This week? We've taken half pay for a fortnight—

CORA: And it's Christmas tomorrow!

BRYCE: Sorry, kid. Santa Claus dropped his sack at Randwick.

HAROLD: Not quite fair, old boy. Business has been slow—

TEXAS: Like all the nags you've been backing.

HAROLD: I paid what I could last week, I'll do the same tonight.

He begins handing out money to all.

DIAMANTINA: Two whole quid. Hubba-hubba.

HAROLD: I'll square you by the end of January. We've got solid dates in Dubbo, Parkes, Orange, Bathurst. There's good money in those towns.

BRYCE: Not to mention good bookies. Pack up, kids. The Western Mail goes through at five past twelve. We'll be back in town for Christmas dinner.

The RINELLIS *go.* BRYCE *goes on packing.*

HAROLD: I can't lose the best troupe of pros I've ever known. Magda, my exotic little songbird, all the way from war-torn—

MAGDA: Coogee. And I'm heading back to Mum's tonight. Coming, Cecil?

MAGDA *goes.*

CECIL: Sorry, Harold. Sorry, Ruby. But if it's you or Maggie—

He runs out.

HAROLD: Cora! Diamantina! The priceless Price Sisters—

DIAMANTINA: No, darling. We work cheap, but not this cheap. [*She pockets her two quid.*] Merry Christmas all. Come on, Cora.

CORA: Mr Slocum, I'll miss you. Joycie, you're gorgeous...

She hugs JOY.

Johnny, you're a big sweetie...

She hugs him.

And Mrs Slocum...

RUBY: Yes, pet, I'm a frigging marvel. Don't miss your train.

CORA *follows* DIAMANTINA.

HAROLD: Texas! This is only a hiccough in the gullet of life.

TEXAS: Hiccoughs always tell me I'm hungry.

She goes. BRYCE *closes his trunk.*

BRYCE: Look after yourself, Joycie. We had some corker times, eh darling?

JOY: If you say so.

BRYCE *goes.* TEXAS *returns with her bag and kisses* HAROLD.

TEXAS: Harold, it's been fun, but—

HAROLD: You all know I'm a gambling man. I'll get back that winning streak—

TEXAS: When you do, give us a yell. Chookas, all.

She goes.

HAROLD: Oh, ye of little faith! Deserting me on the brink of the best year we could ever see! This could break a man's heart—

RUBY: If he had one.

HAROLD: It's bruised, Rube, bruised by rank ingratitude.

RUBY: Dramatics were never your strong suit, darl. Stick to song-and-dance.

HAROLD: Exactly. We've got the tent waiting for us in Dubbo. They'll love the new show. A returned soldier on the bill, and a Victory Parade to close the first half. Has George Sorlie got that?

JOY: No, Sorlie's got twenty-five people on stage. And a band. And money to pay them.

Train whistle.

JOHNNY: Five past twelve. Merry Christmas, all.

RUBY: Time to head home, kids.

HAROLD: And let them think Slocum's is on the skids? We stay on the road.

RUBY: Harold? After what's just happened? You need your head read.

JOY: She's right, Dad.

RUBY: If you think I'm going to turn around... and... and...

She grabs her bag and heads off.

HAROLD: What did you say?

RUBY: Pack the truck. We're going back to Sydney.

HAROLD: Turn around... Turn around!

She turns to him.

No. You said—

RUBY: I said we're going home. Unless you've got a better idea.

She heads off again, followed by JOHNNY *and* JOY.

HAROLD: Oh, I have. A beautiful idea. And it came straight from you.

They stop.

Like I always say, Rube. It's all in the timing.

JOY: This better be good.

HAROLD: Oh, it's better than good.

WHAT IF WE'VE LOST A COUPLE OF PIKERS?
Eh?

WHAT IF THE LESSER LIGHTS HAVE GONE OFF?
THEY'LL BE THE LOSERS, WE'RE THE WINNERS!
BEGINNERS, AND THE SHOW GOES ON...

RUBY: WHAT IF IT'S CHRISTMAS, AND WE'RE STARVING?
Eh?

JOY: WHAT IF THE NEW YEAR'S LOOKING WAN?

JOHNNY: AND WHAT IF WE KNOW THE SHOW'S A GONER?

HAROLD: MY MONOGRAM'S 'THE SHOW GOES ON'.

RUBY: GOES ON?

HAROLD: Yes, this show goes on... regardless.

RUBY: But Harold, where? No, don't tell me. Come on, kids!

HAROLD: Turnaround.

RUBY: When will you stop saying that!

HAROLD: When you stop and listen! This town I know, a good, open, friendly town, can't be far from here, just a few hours west. I see myself spending Christmas there, resting up, no! Working up another act, an act to knock their socks off! That's where I'm heading. Are you coming too? Your choice.

JOY: No choice. I'm skint.

JOHNNY: Me too.

HAROLD *opens his wallet and searches it.*

HAROLD: What have I got here? Abracadabra... My last fiver. That'll get you back to town. Off you go, Joycie. No hard feelings, Johnny-cake. [*He holds the money out.*] Rube, here are the keys to the truck. [*He holds the keys out.*] I can always thumb a ride west.

They look at each other. RUBY *puts her bag down.*

JOHNNY: You sure about this town?

HAROLD: You've been there, son. Turnaround Creek.

RUBY: I've never played Turnaround Creek.

HAROLD: Before your time. An oasis in the West, with a big old pub called the Shamrock. Remember, kids? Just after your mum shot

through. Lovely people, welcomed us with open arms. And they'll
do it again.

JOY: Till they find we can't pay the bill.

HAROLD: We can always pay the bill.

> WE'VE BEEN ON OUR UPPERS
> AND SUNG FOR OUR SUPPERS
> FROM TAMWORTH TO BOURKE TO OBERON,
> AND TURNAROUND CREEK'LL RUN SWEETER THAN
> TREACLE,
> TOMORROW WE CROSS THE RUBICON,
> WE'LL SHOW THE WORLD WE KNOW
> THE SHOW GOES ON!

RUBY/JOY/JOHNNY: AND ON, AND ON, AND ON AND ON...

> *They pick up their bags. He pockets the fiver and leads them off.*

SCENE TWO

Outside the Shamrock Hotel, Turnaround Creek. PEG HARTIGAN *sweeps
the verandah.* MICK HARTIGAN *rolls a smoke.* CLARRIE NUGENT *comes from
the street.*

CLARRIE: Mick. Peg.

PEG: Morning, Clarrie.

CLARRIE: How's the head this morning?

PEG: NOTHIN' DOIN',

> BARRY DOYLE *comes out of the hotel.*

> NOTHIN' DOIN'.

BARRY: We're two for eighty-seven. Morning, Clarrie.

CLARRIE: Morning, Barry. Backing anything?

BARRY: Anything worth backing?

> NOTHIN' DOIN'.

> CLARRIE *hands him the form guide.* PEG *sweeps.*

PEG: Move, Dad. Move, Clarrie. Move, Mick.

Greg Stone (left) as Barry and Greg Saunders as Clarrie in the 1983 NIDA production in Sydney. (Photo: Peter Holderness)

BARRY *moves.* CLARRIE *moves.* MICK *doesn't.*

PEG/MICK/CLARRIE/BARRY: BOXING DAY IN TURNAROUND CREEK,
    NOTHIN' DOIN',
    ONE MORE DAY IN TURNAROUND CREEK,
    NOTHIN' DOIN', NOTHIN' DOIN'.

BARRY: Five bob each way on Greased Lightning.

CATHY *enters from the hotel.*

CATHY: What's happening today? Anything?

BARRY: What does it look like?

CATHY: I woke up with this feeling. Something's going to happen.

MICK: On Boxing Day?

BARRY: BOXING DAY IN TURNAROUND CREEK,

ALL: NOTHIN' DOIN'.

CLARRIE: STATE OF PLAY IN TURNAROUND CREEK,

ALL: NOTHIN' DOIN', NOTHIN' DOIN'.

RED *and* LORNA FARRELL *enter. She is heavily pregnant. Other* TOWNSPEOPLE *may follow.*

LORNA: Oh, my ankles. Morning, Dad.

RED: How we getting on, Barry?

BARRY: Two for eighty-seven, last I heard. Didn't know you were coming in this morning.

He goes inside. Other TOWNSPEOPLE *appear, all somewhat the worse for wear.*

RED: Lorna reckons today's the day.

LORNA: I woke up with this feeling.

CATHY: Me too.

PEG: Lorna, you woke up yesterday with the same feeling, and the day before.

LORNA: But today's the day, I hope.

BARRY *returns.*

BARRY: Three for eighty-seven.

ALL: BOXING DAY IN TURNAROUND CREEK,
    NOTHIN' DOIN'.

CLARRIE: SLOW DECAY IN TURNAROUND CREEK,

ALL: NOTHIN' DOIN', NOTHIN' DOIN'.

MICK: NOTHIN' RISIN' BUT THE DUST,

RED: NOTHIN' STIRRIN' BUT THE FLIES,

WOMEN: NOTHIN' SPREADIN' BUT THE RUST,

ALL: NOTHIN' COMIN' ON AS THE OLD YEAR DIES.

RENIE MCKENNA *enters with loaves of bread.*

CATHY: Auntie Renie, look at them. Like the whole place was dead. Can't you make them do something?

RENIE: They're doing something, Cath. Nursing their heads from last night.

CATHY: Let's make something happen.

PEG: What did you have in mind?

CATHY: I don't know. A picnic?

RENIE: Not exactly picnic weather, love.

CATHY: There's always a hundred reasons to do nothing.

ALL: BOXING DAY IN TURNAROUND CREEK…
         DAY TO DAY IN TURNAROUND CREEK…

BARRY: THE WILLOWS DRAGGLE, THE SHE-OAKS SIGH,

RED: AND BY THE CREEKBED THE SPRING LAMBS DIE,

PEG: THE WESTERLY DRIVES AND THE SUN SITS HIGH.

ALL: [*variously*] NOTHIN' DOIN', NOTHIN' DOIN', NOTHIN' DOIN', NOTHIN' DOIN'.

BARRY: I'll do something. I'll give these poor coves a drink.

He goes inside.

PEG: That's a novel idea.

MICK: You got a better one?

RENIE: Lorna Farrell, you get in out of this heat. Come on, I'll give your feet a rub.

LORNA: Thanks, Auntie Reen. I feel that heavy, either it's twins, or it's coming with luggage.

All follow BARRY *inside.* CATHY *lingers.*

PEG: Cheer up, Cath. Won't always be like this.

CATHY: Won't it?

PEG: Come and give us a hand with dinner.

MISS MAISIE TRENGROVE *approaches.*

CATHY: Hey! Look out there. What is it?

PEG: Could be a bit of weather! No, it's just dust.

MAISIE: No, it's a truck.

CATHY: And it's heading this way!

PEG: You sure?

CATHY: Yes! Whose is it?

PEG: I dunno, but it's dying underneath them.

MAISIE: Are they going to make it over the bridge? No. No. Yes!

CATHY: It's got a name painted on the side.

PEG: I can't read it for dust. Can you, Maisie?

CATHY: They're stopping!

> *Sound of a truck expiring.*

MAISIE: They've got no choice.

CATHY: Who are they?

PEG: Better ask them.

> JOY *and* RUBY *approach, dusty and bedraggled.*

JOY: This is it. The Shamrock Hotel!

RUBY: Thank Christ. Hello, I'm Ruby Slocum. You won't remember me, I wasn't here last time, but you will remember Joy. My stepdaughter, but everyone takes us for sisters. How are you off for rooms? After two nights in that truck I'll sleep anywhere, if you know what I mean.

> *Silence. She mutters to* JOY.

It's a slow Monday night in Cessnock.

MAISIE: Slocum's Tent Show. Clean family fun under canvas. Welcome back to Turna, Miss Slocum.

PEG: When were you here before?

JOY: I was about so high. I tap-danced on the bar.

> JOHNNY *appears with bags.*

Do you remember Johnny?

PEG: Johnny? I think I do…

> LORNA *and* RENIE *and* OTHERS *come out.*

Renie? Lorna? Do you remember these people?

CATHY: It says 'Slocum's Tent Show, Harold Slocum, Prop.'.

> HAROLD *enters.*

Are you the prop?

HAROLD: Yes, young lady, I'm the prop. Harold Slocum at your service.

LORNA: Slocum's Tent Show…

PEG: You had your tent up by the creek.

RENIE: This time there's no creek.

RUBY: This time there's no tent.

JOHNNY: And almost no troupe.

HAROLD: There is a family of tip-top pro's.

PEG: What happened?

RUBY: What happened? What happened? Christmas Eve we had… a fire.

JOY: Yes. Everything up in flames.

HAROLD: No lives lost. And we still have a show.

CATHY: Clean family fun under canvas. Will you do us a show?

MAISIE: I have the key to the School of Arts. You'll be very welcome. I'll go and dust off the piano.

> *She goes.*

PEG: First we'd better find you some rooms. Dad? Dad!

HAROLD: My God, you're Nancy's daughters! I could pick it.

PEG: Peg… Lorna… and Cathy.

HAROLD: Three daughters. I remember two, two little girls, the image of your mother. And where's she? Where's mine hostess? Where's Nancy Doyle?

LORNA: Our mother's dead, Mr Slocum.

PEG: Please, come inside and—

HAROLD: Dead? No! I… I'm sorry. Very sorry.

> BARRY *comes out followed by* MICK, RED *and* CLARRIE *and perhaps other* MEN *of the town.*

Barry? Barry Doyle? It's Harold, Harold Slocum. Slocum's Tent Show. Remember?

> HAROLD *offers his hand.*

CATHY: Their truck's broken down, but Miss Trengrove's going to give them the key to the School of Arts—

PEG: First we're going to find them some rooms!

BARRY: We got no rooms. Mick, give them a hand with their truck. Get them on their way.

HAROLD: Barry...

BARRY: You're not welcome under this roof. None of you.

CATHY: Dad! You got to let them stay!

BARRY: Get inside, Cath. Did you hear me?

> CATHY *goes inside.* BARRY *follows.*

HAROLD: Barry! I'll go and sort this out.

> MICK *bars his way.*

MICK: Nothing to sort out.

HAROLD: Look, Miss Doyle—

MICK: Mrs Hartigan. Let's have a look at this truck...

> *He goes towards it.*

HAROLD: Mrs Hartigan. Will you help us, please?

PEG: I'd like to, but... I'm sorry. Mick will get your truck going.

> *She goes inside.* LORNA *follows* RED *in.*

RENIE: I don't know what's got into that fellow. You wouldn't remember me, but I'm Nancy's sister.

HAROLD: I can see the likeness. She was the first one to greet us, wiped her hands on her apron and ushered us inside. And on New Year's Eve, she danced in a yellow dress.

RENIE: Did she? She was a lovely dancer. Well... I'm sorry about...

> HAROLD *pulls a flower from behind her ear, presenting it to her.*

Oh. Ta. If you need anything for the road, I'm over yonder, in the general store.

> RENIE *goes. The* TROUPE *are alone.*

RUBY: Harold, have you always been this big on the western circuit?

JOY: Give it a rest, Rube.

RUBY: All that blarney on the way here—

HAROLD: Shut up, will you? Give a man a chance to think!

RUBY: Will you think us up a room, or even a bit of food? I'd like one square meal between now and 1946.

HAROLD: Then bite off your tongue and chew on that.

RUBY: This is the end of the road, Harold. I stuck by you when they ran us out of Ipswich, when the Mighty Midgets did us over in Kempsey, when Rudolph the Rubber Man went up on a morals charge in Maitland. I covered when Bo the Wonder Dog dropped dead on stage. And two nights ago, I swallowed all pride and all sense, and trailed you like a mug. But I've followed the drum for the last time. Look at us. No food, no shelter, no transport, and, oh Christ, it's going to rain.

Thunder. MICK *runs on from the truck.* RED *runs out of the pub. He gazes at the lowering sky.*

MICK: Crikey!

MAISIE *returns with other* TOWNSPEOPLE.

MAISIE: Will you look at that?

RED: Look at it? Stand in it!

LORNA *runs out from the pub.* RED *embraces her.*

LORNA: Send 'er down, Hughie!

BARRY, CLARRIE, RENIE, CATHY *and the rest of the* TOWN *return.* RED *kneels on the ground, hat upturned.*

RED: SEND 'ER DOWN, HUGHIE,
             LET THE DRY EARTH DRINK SWEET WATER,

MICK: SEND 'ER DOWN, HUGHIE,
             TILL THE RIVERS FLOW.

BARRY: SEND 'ER DOWN, HUGHIE,
             LEAVE THE GATES OF HEAVEN OPEN,

CLARRIE: SEND 'ER DOWN, HUGHIE,

TOWN MEN: MAKE THE PASTURES GROW.

TOWN WOMEN: SEND 'ER DOWN IN BUCKETS,
             FILL THE BILLABONGS, FILL THE TANKS,
             LET 'ER COME, AND KEEP ON COMING
             TILL TURNAROUND CREEK HAS BURST ITS BANKS.

ALL: SEND 'ER DOWN, HUGHIE,
             TILL THE TROUGHS ARE RUNNING OVER,
             SEND 'ER DOWN, HUGHIE, WASH THE DUSTY TOWN.

SEND 'ER DOWN, HUGHIE, BRING ON LUCERNE, BRING
    ON CLOVER,
SEND 'ER DOWN, HUGHIE, HUGHIE, SEND 'ER DOWN.
SEND 'ER DOWN IN BUCKETS, FILL THE BILLABONGS, FILL
    THE TANKS,
LET 'ER COME, AND KEEP ON COMING
TILL TURNAROUND CREEK HAS BURST ITS BANKS.
SEND 'ER DOWN, HUGHIE,
LET THE DRY EARTH DRINK SWEET WATER,
SEND 'ER DOWN, HUGHIE,
TILL THE RIVERS FLOW.
SEVEN YEARS THE LAND WAS BROWN;
GREEN IT, CLEAN IT, SEND 'ER DOWN,
HUGHIE, SEND 'ER DOWN.

Elise Greig (left) as Joy and Geraldine Turner as Ruby in the 1997 Queensland Theatre Company production in Brisbane. (Photo: Rob MacColl)

TIME TO GIVE THANKS NOW, SEE THE GATES OF HEAVEN
    OPEN;
TIME TO GIVE THANKS NOW, SOON THE GRASS WILL
    GROW;
TIME TO GIVE THANKS NOW, SEE THE DRY EARTH DRINK
    SWEET WATER;
TIME TO GIVE THANKS NOW, TURNAROUND CREEK IN
    FULL FLOW:
THANK YOU.
SEND 'ER DOWN, HUGHIE, SEVEN YEARS WE'VE ALL BEEN
    WAITING,
WE WON'T DROWN, HUGHIE, WE'RE TOO BUSY
    CELEBRATING;
SEVEN YEARS THE LAND WAS BROWN;
GREEN IT, CLEAN IT, SEND 'ER DOWN,
HUGHIE, SEND 'ER DOWN!

The SHOWIES *are taken into the Shamrock.*

SCENE THREE

Inside the Shamrock. A washing line.

JOHNNY: Here we are. Saved by the rain.

PEG: You could say.

JOHNNY: Peggy Doyle… Hartigan. I do remember you from last time.

PEG: 'Course you do.

JOHNNY: You showed me where to find yabbies. Took me to the swimming-hole. We swung on an old tire over the water.

PEG: There's been no swimming round here for years.

JOHNNY: Looks like your luck's changed.

PEG: If this lasts. Give us that.

She offers a clean drab shirt as JOHNNY *sheds his wet one.*

JOHNNY: Snazzy.

PEG: It's my husband's.

He puts it on. She's going.

JOHNNY: You've got beautiful eyes, anyone ever tell you that?

PEG: Yes, once. A traveller from Mark Foy's. My husband decked him. I better get back behind the bar.

JOHNNY: What's the rush?

PEG: Look who's talking.

JOHNNY: Steady on. We were pals last time, Peg.

PEG: We were kids. I'm an old married woman now.

JOHNNY: Even a married woman needs friends.

PEG: You're an expert on married women? Well, this one don't need no trouble from you, Mister Slocum.

JOHNNY: Johnny. As in Johnny-cake. Sweet and wholesome.

PEG: And a bit overdone.

They laugh as MICK *enters, followed by* CATHY.

MICK: Your truck's working all right, mate.

JOHNNY: Oh. Good-oh.

MICK: Only now she's bogged in. Not that you'd get out anyway. Creek's up over the bridge. Is that my shirt?

JOHNNY: It's certainly not mine. Thanks.

He goes.

MICK: Bar's starting to fill up.

PEG: I'll be down in a tick. I'll just soak this for him.

MICK: Don't go overboard.

PEG: They're guests, Mick.

MICK: Guests pay. This mob are reffos.

He goes.

CATHY: I like them being here, Peg. Don't you?

PEG: SOMETHING ON THE WIND,
SOMETHING STIRRING,
SOMETHING ON THE WIND SHAKES THE WINDOWPANE.
SOMETHING ON THE WIND
TO STIR THE DUSTY CORNERS,
SOMETHING NEW ON THE WIND WITH THE RAIN.

Verandah, or street.

HAROLD: Miss Trengrove?

MAISIE: Mr Slocum.

HAROLD: You were kind enough to offer us the School of Arts Hall.

MAISIE: You were kind enough to offer us a show. I believe Turna's good and ready now. Step this way...

> BARRY *appears with* RENIE.

BARRY: Maisie? Maisie Trengrove!

MAISIE: Not now, Barry. I'm about to show Mr Slocum the facilities. He's going to give us a night to remember.

> *She opens her umbrella.* HAROLD *escorts* MAISIE *down the street.*

BARRY: They're not putting on no show.

RENIE: I don't see how you can stop them, Barry.

BARRY: I can stay away. And any friend of mine will do likewise.

RENIE: Oh, malarky! I'll be there. I'm dying for a good laugh. I reckon we all are.

BARRY: What if the laugh's on us?

RENIE: Crikey, what's your problem? Bit of bad blood between you and Slocum? Forget about it.

BARRY: I don't forget nothing, Reen.

RENIE: Then if you'll tell me what the bloody hell's going on—

> *He's gone.*

> > SOMETHING ON THE WIND WITH THE STRANGERS,
> > SOMETHING ON THE WIND SPINS THE WEATHERVANE,
> > SOMETHING NEW AND STRANGE, AND ALL THE TOWN IS STIRRING,
> > SOMETHING FRESH ON THE WIND WITH THE RAIN.

> *She goes after* BARRY *as* CLARRIE *pursues* JOY *out of the hotel.* CATHY *watches.*

JOY: Watch it, mate.

CLARRIE: You got the wrong end of the stick. Hubba-hubba means—

JOY: How do you do? And the wolf-whistle, what did that mean?

CLARRIE: Sign of admiration. You're very easy on the optic nerve.

JOY: You're the one with nerve, Charlie.

CLARRIE: Close. Clarrie. Clarrie Nugent. Welcome to Turna, Miss Slocum.

JOY: I been here before, remember.

CLARRIE: I remember a curly-head kid dancing on the bar.

JOY: That was me. Baby Joycie, doing the Shirley Temple bit. Sixteen years on, and I'm still at it.

CLARRIE: Only the legs are longer.

JOY: If your tongue gets any longer it'll be dragging on the ground.

CLARRIE: Steady on, Joycie. Soon as I saw you this morning, I knew we had to be friends.

JOY: Friends?

CLARRIE: And that's the way we'll stay. Till you find you can't keep your hands off me. Welcome back, Joycie Slocum.

He tips his hat and goes in as RUBY *hurries out.*

RUBY: A show, he says. And tomorrow night! As though we can just pull something out of the air.

CATHY *appears from nowhere.*

CATHY: We'll find you anything you need. There's a big dress-up box upstairs.

RUBY: That's a huge comfort, dear.

CATHY: I've never seen a show. What will you be doing?

JOY: You wait and see. Which way is the hall?

CATHY: Straight down the street, past Auntie Reen's, right beside the war memorial. I woke up with this feeling. I knew something was bound to happen. I'm real glad you're here.

JOY: So are we, Cathy.

RUBY: 'Course we are. Thrilled to bits.

They go as PEG *pursues* MICK.

PEG: I want you to take me to that show tomorrow, Mick.

MICK: Your dad won't like it, Peggy.

PEG: Then he can lump it. I'm going.

MICK *goes.* BARRY *sees* MAISIE.

BARRY: You shouldn't have done that, Maise. I don't want them here. They'll only bring trouble.

MAISIE: So far they've only brought the rain. Is that your idea of trouble?

They part as JOY *and* RUBY *approach the hall.*

JOY: Turnaround Creek School of Arts, 1901.

RUBY: 1901. Christ. It's as old as... as the century. Showtime again and here I am, struggling into the blue [*or other appropriate colour*] satin.

JOY: You always look lovely in that.

RUBY: That's good. Tomorrow night might be my last hurrah.

They go. CATHY *sees* LORNA.

CATHY: You just got to hold on till after the show.

LORNA: I'm not making any promises. Neither is [*the baby*] this one.

CATHY: What a week! The rain, a show, a baby, then New Year's Eve—

LORNA: And then what?

CATHY: I dunno. Something.

LORNA *goes.*

> SOMETHING ON THE WIND, SOMETHING STARTING,
> SOMETHING ON THE WIND NOTHING CAN EXPLAIN.
> SOMETHING ON THE WIND LIKE CHRISTMAS IN THE STORIES,
> SOMETHING GOOD ON THE WIND WITH THE RAIN.
> ON THE WIND WITH THE RAIN...

TOWNSWOMEN: [*offstage*] SOMETHING ON THE WIND WITH THE STRANGERS,

> SOMETHING ON THE WIND NOTHING CAN EXPLAIN,
> SOMETHING ON THE WIND, AND NOTHING TURNS TO SOMETHING,
> SOMETHING FRESH ON THE WIND WITH THE RAIN,
> ON THE WIND WITH THE RAIN,
> ON THE WIND WITH THE RAIN...
> SOMETHING ON THE WIND...

CATHY *goes.*

SCENE FOUR

On stage, the School of Arts Hall. RUBY *marks a tango with* JOHNNY *and* JOY. MAISIE *plays an old upright piano, guided by* HAROLD.

HAROLD: Come on, Rube. Sing up.

RUBY: Could you try and give it a bit more zip, dear?

> *They see* PEG *and* CATHY *with a bundle of clothes. Behind them hover* CLARRIE, LORNA, RED *and* RENIE *and other* TOWNSPEOPLE.

CATHY: We brought you the dress-up clothes.

JOY: Gorgeous.

RENIE: Peg used to be a princess in this.

JOHNNY: I can see it.

CLARRIE: Go on. We didn't meant to break your stride.

HAROLD: Just a brush-up for tomorrow night. The Slocums go Latin. Hit it, darl. [*Aside, to* RUBY] Free publicity.

RUBY: You'll love this, friends. It was banned in Ipswich.

> THE FRENCH KNOW LOVE AND ITS HISTORY,
> AND THE FEVER OF VIVE L'AMOUR;
> SO WHEN THEY DANCE EACH NIGHT TO ITS MYSTERY
> ONE FATAL RHYTHM IS WITH 'EM ON THE FLOOR.
> OH, WHAT IS THE STEP THAT IGNITES 'EM,
> DELIGHTS 'EM FROM MIDNIGHT UNTIL FOUR?
> NO RHUMBA, OR TWO-STEP,
> BUT THAT JE-VOUS-AIME-BEAUCOUP STEP,
> LE TANGO, TANGO D'AMOUR.
> FOR PASSION SHOULD BURN, NEVER SMOULDER,
> AND WHAT'S BETTER TO SET A HEART ABLAZE?
> CHEEK TO CHEEK, AND SHOULDER TO SHOULDER,
> SLEEK AS SATIN, THAT LATIN QUARTER CRAZE…
> AH, THAT IS THE STEP THAT INFLAMES ME,
> AND CLAIMS ME AS YOUR VICTIM ON THE FLOOR:
> NO CANADIAN THREE-STEP,
> BUT THAT OOH-LA-LA-MAIS-OUI STEP,
> LE TANGO, TANGO D'AMOUR.

JOY *and* JOHNNY *dance.*

JOY/JOHNNY: YOU WARN ME OF THE DANGER THAT AWAITS ME,
     I'M DRAWN LIKE A MOTH TO YOUR FLAME;
     THE ROSE THAT YOU BITE ON FASCINATES ME.
     SUPPOSE THAT I WHISPER JE T'AIME! JE T'AIME!
RUBY: YOU ARE DANCING THE DANCE THAT ENTICES,
     AND SPICES THE AIR WITH ALLURE:
     NO PERFUME BY CHANEL,
     BUT A FAR MORE POTENT SPELL…
     LE TANGO…
RUBY/JOY/JOHNNY: TANGO D'AMOUR. OLE!

Karen Vickery as Ruby in the 1983 NIDA production in Sydney.
(Photo: Peter Holderness)

Dance break. HAROLD *brings* CLARRIE *and* JOY *together, advances on* RENIE. RUBY *takes on* RED. JOHNNY *offers to dance with* PEG. *She accepts. All four couples dance.* CATHY *applauds. Perhaps she dons some of the dressing-up finery.* RENIE, *breathless and laughing, passes* HAROLD *to* CATHY.

RENIE: Go on, Cath. Have a go.

CATHY *dances with* HAROLD. RENIE *watches them, standing by* MAISIE *at the piano.* MICK *has arrived.*

MICK: That's enough of that. Hey!

MAISIE *stops.* MICK *separates* CATHY *from* HAROLD.

HAROLD: It's just a bit of fun, son.

MICK: Her dad doesn't want her here.

RENIE: Oh, for God's sake—

MICK: Peg, get her home. I said get her home, did you hear me?

PEG: Yes, Mick, but I'm not some old cattle dog.

JOHNNY: What's she doing wrong?

MICK: Her dad wants her home. Take it up with him.

He goes.

PEG: We better go, Cath.

CATHY: No.

RED: You'll only be in worse strife.

RENIE: Come on. I'm sorry, Mr Slocum.

HAROLD: Never mind. Tomorrow night you'll sit out there, we'll be up here, and you'll see the whole shebang.

LORNA, PEG, CATHY, RENIE *and* RED *go,* CLARRIE *last.*

RUBY: What the hell are we playing at! They don't want us here.

MAISIE: We need you here, Mrs Slocum. Don't be put off. And tomorrow night I'll give it all the zip in the world.

She goes.

HAROLD: Let's mark through 'The End of the Parade'.

JOHNNY: I could do that in my sleep!

HAROLD: No, son, now we're going to close with it—

RUBY: With a ballad!

HAROLD: We've got the Victory banners. We'll march on and join you, formation salute, and final tableau. A big, bright finish—

JOHNNY: Four of us, that's a big finish?

HAROLD: Hey! You know the drill, Johnny-cake. On this stage—

JOHNNY: Your word is law. Not today, Harold. I need a drink.

JOY: It'll be right on the night, Dad.

HAROLD: Not if we don't make it right!

RUBY: When has he ever let you down, Harold?

HAROLD: How about the day he went and joined up?

JOY: I'd almost swear you meant that.

JOHNNY: He does. Come on.

>   *He and* JOY *go.* HAROLD *starts rehearsing.*

RUBY: Slocum's Tent Show. Clean family fun under water. Listen to it, pelting down. No one's going to come out in that.

HAROLD: You want to bet? Place will be jam-packed tomorrow night. We'll make a motser. 'Friends, this is no ordinary town…'

RUBY: Who is it this time? Renie McKenna, the grocer's widow?

HAROLD: 'This is Turnaround Creek! And speaking of Turnaround…'

RUBY: Is it someone younger? Is it Peg? You always had a good line in barmaids.

HAROLD: 'Speaking of Turnaround, we've got something that'll get you up if you're down, over if you're under…'

RUBY: Harold, look at me! We could have gone back to Sydney. Why in the name of God did you bring us here? Hallie, why?

HAROLD: Because this place had something once. And I came looking for it.

RUBY: For something? Or someone?

HAROLD: Yes, Ruby, for someone.

RUBY: I knew it.

HAROLD: Someone named Harold Slocum.

RUBY: Oh. I remember him. If you find him, give him a message, will you? There's someone else looking for him. Someone who's trailed him through a lot of other towns. Tell him she'd like to catch up with him. And pretty soon, 'cause she's running out of puff.

>   *She goes.*

HAROLD: 'Friends, this is no ordinary town, this is Turnaround Creek, and speaking of Turnaround…'

> WINKS TO THE FRONT ROW, GLANCES IN THE MAIN STREET,
> SLOCUM ON A PROMISE, HEAVEN ON A PLATE;
> A NEW NAME, A NEW FACE, GOT HER? FORGET HER!
> THE GLAD EYE WORKS EVERY TIME, EVERY DATE…
> TILL ONE MORNING I STAND ON A HOTEL VERANDAH,
> OUT FOR A PROMISE, A WINK OR A GLANCE;
> ALL THAT I SEE IS A LONG STEADY STARE,
> BLUE EYES THAT SHONE BENEATH BRIGHT COPPER HAIR,
> ALL THAT I SEE IS THE MORNING
> IN THOSE EYES, THE EYES OF NANCY DOYLE.

SCENE FIVE

Behind the pub. PEG *has a case of spirits.* JOHNNY *pursues her.*

PEG: Mister, whatever you're after—

JOHNNY: I'm not after anything. I'd like to get to know you.

PEG: That's a good line. I suppose it works like a charm every time, every town?

JOHNNY: Fair enough, it's an old line. Give me a sec to think up a new one. Tell me about Peg Hartigan. I mean it.

PEG: Nothing much to tell.

JOHNNY: Tons of things. What's your favourite smell? What's your favourite song? Did Mick always have a gammy leg? Or is it a war wound?

> *She nods.*

When was your last pay packet? Or do you have to ask Barry for money? Even a few bob to buy a length of fabric off a traveller?

PEG: Been a long time since I bought anything off a traveller. There's been no money for extras, Johnny. We got enough IOUs in the till to stuff a mattress.

JOHNNY: What's in the locket? Have you ever been drunk? Have you ever been up in an aeroplane?

PEG: An aeroplane? How about a rocket to the moon?

JOHNNY: When you laugh, you look like a different woman.

PEG: Maybe. But she's married too. I have to get back to work.

JOHNNY: Let me carry that [grog] for you.

PEG: And walk in with me? I'd never hear the end of it. You follow me at a distance, and keep your eyes off me.

JOHNNY: End of the night, I'll be waiting.

PEG: You'll be waiting a ruddy long time.

> *She returns to the bar. A party is in progress. All the* TOWNSPEOPLE *are there.*

CLARRIE: This has been a shocking day for Turnaround Creek.

MAISIE: I beg your pardon, Clarence!

CLARRIE: We haven't had a Test score since lunchtime! This wretched rain has put the wireless on the blink.

BARRY: Mick'll fix it.

CLARRIE: And the telephone's down. How's a man supposed to do his business?

RENIE: Stop your whingeing, Clarrie, and give us a toast.

CLARRIE: That ought to be Barry's job.

BARRY: A toast? I give you the end of a drought—

> HAROLD *and* JOHNNY *come in from the street.*

RED: And here they are, the mob that brought the rain!

HAROLD: All in a day's work. This round's on me, Peg. Put it on my bill.

> *Drinks are handed around.*

MAISIE: But nobody drink till we've made a toast! Barry boy, you were cut off in mid-flow.

> BARRY *says nothing.*

Someone else, then, quick sticks.

LORNA: Go on, Red.

RED: Me? Well… it's been hard, eh? A hard haul for all and sundry. Six years of war, four or five years of service for some blokes, and some came home, some didn't…

He glances at RENIE. *She raises her glass. Perhaps Col McKenna's name is murmured?*

... and us on the land, we've had our own battles to fight. Eh, Lorn? Seven years we've watched our dams dry up and our pastures disappear, we've cut back on stock because we had nothing to graze them on, we've seen a prize herd turn to skin and bone. But now! Crikey, listen to that drumming on the roof! Anyway... I give you the good years ahead!

> *All join the toast.*

RENIE: I give you the showies!

> *All join the toast. They drink.* HAROLD *takes* CLARRIE *aside.*

HAROLD: Small matter of business, Clarrie.

CLARRIE: Music to my ears, old son.

HAROLD: Eagle Farm, New Year's Eve, the Golden Slipper. Would there be a beast named Rainbow Gal in the running?

CLARRIE: Rainbow Gal? That's a new one on me.

> *He checks the form-guide and whistles.*

Yep. There she is, squire. Fifty to one.

HAROLD: A fiver to win.

RUBY: A fiver!

HAROLD: Yes, Ruby. [*To* CLARRIE] Long odds, I grant you, but I'm on a hunch here, Clarrie.

CLARRIE: All we got to go on in this world, son.

> RUBY *watches the cash change hands.*

RUBY: It is now.

RENIE: Mr Slocum! How about a song?

> BARRY *glares at her.* HAROLD *sees.*

HAROLD: We'll give you plenty of songs tomorrow night. I got a better idea. Lend us a quid, Rube?

> *She glares at him, then does.*

A fiddly for the best joke of the night. And they're racing!

RED: DID YOU HEAR THE ONE ABOUT THE FIVE-LEGGED DONKEY?

SOMEONE: Yes.

RENIE: DID YOU HEAR THE ONE ABOUT THE DRUNKARD AND THE NUN?

SOMEONE: Yes.

CLARRIE: DID YOU HEAR THE ONE ABOUT THE FROG AND THE VICAR?

ALL: Yes.

          THE LANDLORD JOKE? HEARD THAT ONE?

RED: Which one?

CLARRIE: This one. Bloke goes to his landlord, says: 'I've got a leak in my sink.' The landlord says: 'Why not? Everybody else does.'

Laughter. HAROLD *waves the pound note.*

ALL: [*as assigned*] HEAR ABOUT THE DROVER WITH THE MANGY SHEEPDOG?

          HEAR ABOUT THE JACKAROO THAT HAD A WOODEN LEG?

          TOMMY AND PADDY AND JOCK ARE ON A TROOPSHIP—

          THERE'S A FRENCH COCKATOO THAT SAYS—

A rude punch-line is whispered among the BLOKES. RED *guffaws.*

          THIS ACTRESS MEETS A BISHOP ON A DESERT ISLAND—

          THIS TEXAN ASKS A POLAR BEAR TO DANCE—

          A SALESMAN CALLS ON THE FARMER'S DAUGHTER—

          SHE'S IN THE ALTOGETHER AND HE SAYS—

Another tag among the BLOKES. RED *guffaws louder.*

          THIS POM TURNS UP ON THE FIRST DAY OF SHEARING—

          THIS PROZZIE SEES A COPPER ON THE BEAT—

          THE SWAGGIE TAKES A LOOK AT THE FLY-BLOWN DAMPER—

          STIFFY LOOKS AT MO, AND HE SAYS—

MAISIE *has planted herself among the* MEN. *She hears this tag and hoots.*

ALL: [*as assigned*] HEAR ABOUT THE CATTLE DOG WHOSE EARS TURN PURPLE?

          HEAR ABOUT THE CHIMPANZEE THAT LEARNS TO TALK?

          HEAR ABOUT THE PLUMBER WITH THE SEPTIC FINGER?

From left back row: Todd Boyce, Ritchie Singer, Dean Nottle, Julie Haseler, Greg Saunders, Paul Keane; front row: Lyn Pierse, Terence Clarke and Andrew Lloyde in the 1983 NIDA production. (Photo: Peter Holderness)

From left: Rebecca Riggs, Geraldine Turner, Melissa McMahon (kneeling), Bev Shean and Bille Brown in the 1997 Queensland Theatre Company production. (Photo: Rob MacColl)

HEAR ABOUT THE WAITER WITH THE DIRTY FORK?
HEAR ABOUT THE MULLYGRUBBER AT THE 'GABBA?
HEAR ABOUT THE COCKY FINDS A TEENAGE BRIDE?
HEAR ABOUT THE SQUATTER WITH THE TALKING HEIFER?
HEAR ABOUT THE SAILOR-BOY WHOSE BERTH'S TOO WIDE?

ALL: [overlapping, as assigned] HEAR ABOUT THE WALLABY—
HEAR ABOUT THE MAMA'S BOY—
HEAR ABOUT THE LORIKEET—
HEAR ABOUT THE CRICKETER—
HEAR ABOUT THE USHERETTE WHO MEETS BEN CHIFLEY—
HE SAYS WHAT ABOUT—
SHE SAYS WHAT ABOUT—

ALL: HERE'S ANOTHER, HAVE ANOTHER, JUST ONE MORE, MATE!
GET THAT? GOT THAT? WHAT DO YOU THINK!
STOP ME IF— TOP ME UP— THIS'LL KILL YOU!
WAIT TILL I— WHAT ABOUT— HAVE ANOTHER DRINK!

Nearly all are drunk.

RED: This one's for Lorna!
HANG ON! I'VE GOT... THIS'LL KILL YOU!
STOP ME IF... LORNA, LISTEN TO THIS!
HEAR ABOUT THE DISTRICT NURSE THAT CAN'T STOP FARTING!

LORNA cracks up, then starts to groan.

LORNA: Red, quick, get me upstairs!

RED and PEG assist her.

RENIE: I'm right behind you, darling!

She and MAISIE follow them out.

CLARRIE: Reckon your quid's safe, Harold.

HAROLD reaches for it. RUBY snatches it and goes.

I dunno, drought-breaking, baby-making. Beats pulling a rabbit out of a hat.

CLARRIE follows JOY into the street. The other TOWNSPEOPLE go, leaving HAROLD alone in the bar with MICK.

HAROLD: So Barry's going to be a grandfather. First time.

> MICK *nods.*

You and Peggy haven't got round to it yet?

> MICK *shakes his head. He turns a light out.*

Last drinks? I'll just—

> MICK *has gone.* HAROLD*'s alone.*

Finish this.

> HAROLD *drains his glass. He finds* BARRY *in the street.*

You're going to be a grandfather. You pleased?

> BARRY *nods.*

A big night for Turnaround Creek.

BARRY: You could say. You spun some good yarns in there.

HAROLD: Thanks.

BARRY: Funny you kept the best one to yourself. I'm sure it's won you
a quid in some bar in some other town.

> THERE'S A LAUGHING WOMAN AT A NEW YEAR DANCE,
> SHE WEARS A YELLOW DRESS, SHE'S BEAUTIFUL.
> STRANGER TAKES A SHINE TO HER CLEAR BLUE EYES,
> DANCES WITH HER CLOSE TILL SHE STINKS OF
> BRILLIANTINE.
> STOP ME IF YOU'VE HEARD IT, THIS ONE'S A KILLER:
> HE TAKES HER OUTSIDE WHERE THE GRASS IS WET WITH
> RAIN.
> SHE COMES BACK IN WITH HER YELLOW DRESS MUDDY;
> AND AFTER THAT NIGHT SHE NEVER LAUGHED AGAIN.

HAROLD: You knew all along.

BARRY: Not till after you'd gone. If I'd known before, I would have
taken you apart. Why have you come back?

HAROLD: This town gave me something once. I need it again, Barry.
I'm a desperate man.

BARRY: You're a dead man if you're not out of here the minute the
creek drops.

HAROLD: You don't know the whole story.

> RUBY *enters unobserved.*

BARRY: I know the way it ended. Nancy died.

HAROLD: Yes. That was cruel. A woman as lovely as that...

BARRY: Shut your dirty mouth!

> *He takes a swing at* HAROLD *who squares up to him. They fight.* RUBY *has to separate them.*

RUBY: Stop it, the both of you! [*To* HAROLD] Nancy. This is new. I've seen you chasing all kinds of women, but never a dead one.

HAROLD: Get out of here.

RUBY: You get. I want to talk to him. Go on!

> HAROLD *goes.*

Nancy. Of course. Dancing out here in a yellow dress.

> BARRY *starts to go.*

Tell me about her.

BARRY: Why?

RUBY: Because he came back for her. That makes her different from all the others.

BARRY: All the others? Have there been that many?

RUBY: Generally only one per town.

BARRY: You're a good-looking woman. Why isn't he happy with you?

RUBY: Was Nancy all that happy with you? Well, was she?

BARRY: Give it a rest, Mrs Slocum.

RUBY: Sorry. That's me, barging in where I'm not wanted. Not that any of us are wanted round here. We'll be out of your way as soon as we can.

> *He's going.*

When did Nancy go?

BARRY: A long time ago.

RUBY: How?

BARRY: She died having Cathy.

RUBY: And you're scared something might go wrong for Lorna? She'll be right. Tell me, which one of them looks most like Nancy?

BARRY: Peggy. She's got the smile. And the eyes. Nancy was...

RUBY: Nancy was. Yes. I can imagine.

> *She goes.*

BARRY: SHE STOOD THERE ONE MORNING ON THE SHAMROCK
VERANDAH,
HAIR BURNISHED COPPER, EYES LIKE THE SEA.
NAME NANCY KEENAN, AGE SEVENTEEN,
STRENGTH IN HER HANDS, BODY STURDY AND LEAN,
EYES THAT REFLECTED THE MORNING,
THAT MORNING, THOSE EYES,
THE EYES OF NANCY KEENAN, THE EYES OF NANCY
DOYLE...
OTHER MORNINGS HAVE BROKEN, OTHER SUNS, OTHER
SKIES;
BUT EACH MORNING WITHOUT HER SOMETHING DIES;
THOUGH EACH NIGHT HAS ITS PASSING,
AND A NEW DAY WILL RISE,
THERE WILL NEVER BE MORNING LIKE THE MORNING IN
HER EYES.

SCENE SIX

Later that night. JOHNNY *waits outside the hotel.* RED *emerges.*

RED: It's a cruel business. Four hours she's been heaving away. And Renie reckons it could easy be another four.

JOHNNY: She'll be right, Red. I'm looking forward to that big cigar.

RED: This is Turna, mate. I'll sling you the makings and you can roll your own.

Sounds within.

Oh, crikey. Fingers crossed.

He goes as MICK *approaches from the street.*

MICK: You're up late. I thought you'd all be stonkered.

JOHNNY: Too much going on. And you're still out and about.

MICK: Been checking the creek. She's still up over the bridge.

JOHNNY: Looks like you're stuck with us for the duration.

MICK: Yeah. For the duration.

He goes. CATHY *finds* JOHNNY.

CATHY: Hey, Johnny Slocum. Will you do me a favour?

JOHNNY: Depends.

CATHY: Where's your dad?

JOHNNY: Upstairs with a bottle of rum, trying to put himself to sleep.

CATHY: No one's going to sleep, not with Lorna screaming up there. Will you ask him to come down and talk to me?

JOHNNY: Go up and knock on his door.

CATHY: I can't. Dad might see me. Please, Johnny. It's life and death.

JOHNNY: Life and death? Whew! All right.

> *He goes.* CATHY *watches as* JOY *and* CLARRIE *come down the street. They dodge a puddle.*

JOY: Watch the puddles.

CLARRIE: Must be a great life, Joycie.

JOY: You reckon? Give me half a chance, I'd throw it in tomorrow.

CLARRIE: Not tomorrow! You promised us a show!

JOY: Yeah, there's always one more show.

CLARRIE: Me, I'd love to give it a go. Reckon I'd be a natural, stepping out like this with a beautiful girl. We got this big empty street. All we need is a band…

> WATCH THE PUDDLES!

JOY: WATCH THE PUDDLES!

CLARRIE: WATCH THE PUDDLES!

> *He watches as* JOY *dances.*

CLARRIE: WHATCHA DOIN'?

JOY: WHATCHA DOIN'?

CLARRIE: WHATCHA DOIN'? I DON'T MEAN TO BE RUDE!

JOY/CLARRIE: THERE'S A CLUE IN TWO IN A DOIN'-IT MOOD.

CLARRIE: WATCH THE PUDDLES!

JOY: JUMP THE PUDDLES!

CLARRIE: DODGE THE PUDDLES,

JOY: STEPPING ELEGANTLY.

CLARRIE: SKIP THE PUDDLES, CUDDLES, COME TRIPPIN' WITH ME.

> *Other* TOWNSPEOPLE *join them.* JOY *and* CLARRIE *relish an audience.*

JOY: WATCH THE PUDDLES,

CLARRIE: BETTER NOT DROWN,

JOY: WATCH THE PUDDLES,

CLARRIE: WASHING THE TOWN,

JOY: WATCH THE PUDDLES, STEPPIN' ELEGANTLY,

CLARRIE: FRED AND GINGER, STEPPING IT OUT ON A SPREE…

CLARRIE/JOY: SKIP THE PUDDLES, CUDDLES, COME TRIPPIN' WITH ME!

ALL: EVERY DRAIN IN TURNAROUND CREEK,
              FLOWS WITH RAIN IN TURNAROUND CREEK,
              NO CONTAININ' TURNAROUND CREEK,
              THE WEATHER'S GONE CRAZY, SO WHY SHOULDN'T WE?

JOY/WOMEN: WATCH THE PUDDLES,

CLARRIE/MEN: OUT IN THE STREET,

JOY/WOMEN: SKIP THE PIDDLES,

CLARRIE/MEN: LIGHT ON YOUR FEET,

Greg Saunders as Clarrie and Julie Haseler as Joy in the 1983 NIDA production in Sydney. (Photo: Peter Holderness)

JOY/WOMEN: JUMP THE PUDDLES,
               YOU'RE SO DEVIL-MAY-CARE!

       CLARRIE *and the* TOWN MEN *whistle.*

ALL: LEAP THE PUDDLES,
               ALL OF US DANCING ON AIR!

       All dance. TOWNSPEOPLE *drift off into the night.*

JOY: GEE, IT'S WET OUT,
CLARRIE: SAY THAT AGAIN!
JOY: GEE, IT'S WET OUT,
CLARRIE: OUT IN THE RAIN,
JOY: COLD AND WET OUT,
CLARRIE: AH-TCHOO!
JOY: AND THIS DRESS IS SO THIN!
CLARRIE: SKIN THE LIZARDS, TWO OF US WET TO THE SKIN!
JOY: IF IT'S WET OUT,
CLARRIE/JOY: GET OUT OF HERE AND GET IN.

       He escorts her inside. CATHY *is alone.* HAROLD *comes out followed by* JOHNNY. *He carries a pack of cards.*

HAROLD: Miss Cathy Doyle, Harold Slocum, here at your bidding. Pick a card, any card. Don't show me.

       She picks one.

CATHY: Have you got room for me?
JOHNNY: In the show?
CATHY: Don't be stupid. In your truck.
HAROLD: Do you have... the Jack of Spades?
CATHY: Yes!
HAROLD: This time, pick two—
CATHY: Listen to me. I have to get out of here.
HAROLD: Take two cards.

       She does.

CATHY: You have to help me. I'm old enough.
JOHNNY: How old?
CATHY: Sixteen.
JOHNNY: Bulldust.

CATHY: Next September. Just give me a ride out. Please?

HAROLD: Two Kings? Hearts and Clubs?

> CATHY *looks. She has the cards.*

Don't you want to stay for the good times? Things are looking up here, poppet.

CATHY: Only 'cause you come. You saw what happened today. I was only having a bit of a dance. He sent Mick for me.

HAROLD: Now take three cards, any three...

CATHY: I copped a belting soon as I got home.

> BARRY *appears from the pub with* MICK.

BARRY: Inside, Cath. Get to bed.

CATHY: Nobody else is in bed, nobody in the whole town.

BARRY: I'm not talking to nobody else, I'm talking to you. Now get inside.

JOHNNY: So you can belt her again?

BARRY: What's it to you, boy?

HAROLD: She's not doing anyone any harm.

MICK: He won't have her hanging round with you mob. And I don't blame him.

JOHNNY: You looking for a fight, pal? 'Cause you got one if you make one more crack like that.

MICK: Yeah?

BARRY: Mick. Settle down. Take the girl inside.

CATHY: I hate you.

BARRY: I'll deal with this inside.

HAROLD: I started this. I don't want her getting into strife—

BARRY: Then keep your distance from all of us.

> *Hubbub inside.* RED *runs out.* MAISIE *and* RENIE *and* OTHERS *are behind him.* RUBY *appears.*

RED: Nancy! Nancy's here! I'm a father! You're a grandfather, Barry boy! Cath, you're an auntie, and Mick, you're an uncle, and Mr Slocum and Mrs Slocum, you're... a couple of beauts.

> *Perhaps* PEG *brings the baby out.*

She's here, she's beautiful, and we'll call her Nancy.

> *All congratulate him and* BARRY.

The drinks are on me. Come on!

All head indoors, BARRY *and* RENIE *last. She takes his arm.*

RENIE: I'm that pleased for you, Barry. I'm glad they named her for Nancy.

BARRY: Can I take a look at her?

RENIE: Of course you can. You can hold her, even.

BARRY: A grandfather. Crikey, I'll have to start growing a beard. Thanks for seeing her through it.

RENIE: I wouldn't have missed it for quids.

BARRY: Can I ask you one more favour?

RENIE: Ask away.

BARRY: Straighten Cathy out. Take her to stay over your place for a few nights.

RENIE: But she's having the time of her life.

BARRY: She can have it some other time. Not now, not with this mob.

RENIE: You've ignored the girl for years. Now you want to bring her into line when the rest of the town is kicking its heels up. If Nancy was here—

BARRY: Well, she's not!

RENIE: Well, if she was...

He's going.

Don't you walk away from me, Barry Doyle. You're not the only one who's lost someone. I miss Col McKenna something chronic, but I get on with life, don't I? Look at you. The blinds are down. That's what Nancy used to say. 'I try to get through to him, but he goes and drops the blinds.'

BARRY: You don't know what you're talking about.

RENIE: Barry, *you* don't know what I'm talking about, and that's half your trouble.

BARRY: Let it go, Reen.

PEG comes out from the hotel with HAROLD.

I'll ask you one last time—

RENIE: And you'll get the same answer: let the poor kid go! I've brought those girls up for you, haven't I? And never said a ruddy word. Now I'm saying *no*.

BARRY: All right, Reen. But we're strangers from now on.

RENIE: Your funeral.

In silence, HAROLD *approaches.*

HAROLD: Barry... allow me to offer my congratulations.

BARRY: Thanks.

RENIE: What about a little drink to celebrate, Mr Slocum? Never let it be said Turna was lacking in hospitality. Step this way.

She takes his arm and goes indoors.

BARRY: Peggy, can I talk to you a minute?

PEG: Not now, Dad.

He goes in. She starts to cry. MICK *comes out.*

MICK: I bet you could do with a drink.

PEG: Did you see her, Mick? Little tiny hands, barely the size of a two-bob bit.

MICK: Look... we'll get round to it in time, Peg. Don't cry, love.

PEG: I'll be right. Will you take me to that show tomorrow?

MICK: I don't go for that stuff.

PEG: How do you know till you give it a go?

MICK: I know one thing. Barry gave the word, said he didn't want us—

PEG: Yes, Barry gave the word! Clicks his fingers and you come to heel like an old kelpie. Never mind what the rest of us want!

MICK: Keep your bloody voice down!

PEG: Don't give me orders. You're the cattle dog, not me.

MICK: Don't push me, Peg, or so help me, I'll—

PEG: You'll what? What!

MICK: Christ. Look, come on inside. They'll be starting to wonder—

PEG: Let them wonder.

He starts to go inside.

Listen, I'm going to that show, with you or without you.

MICK: Suit yourself.

MICK *goes in.* PEG *paces the street. The lights go out. She sees* JOHNNY *in the shadows.*

PEG: I told you not to hang round.

JOHNNY: But I needed to see you. Like you need to see me.

PEG: Got tickets on yourself, haven't you? Give me a smoke.

JOHNNY: You don't look like a smoker.

PEG: I'm not.

>   *He lights her one. She sits.*

Haven't done this since I was a kid. Still tastes like a horse's rear end. Not that I can speak from experience.

>   *He massages her neck and shoulders. She allows it.*

What about the baby, eh? Little Nancy. What a day. Feels more like a week. You know you're the first person to do this for me since my mother? [*She rises.*] That's enough.

JOHNNY: You reckon?

PEG: I can't stay out here.

JOHNNY: Why?

PEG: Starting to rain again.

JOHNNY: We can stand on the verandah.

PEG: No. Someone'll see us.

>   *He kisses her.*

Don't. I have to go.

JOHNNY: No, you don't.

PEG: Oh, I do. [*She goes into the street.*] Feel that. Next Christmas we'll think we dreamt it. Rain coming down in torrents. Main street like a creek, creek like a river. Seven years, we've been waiting.

>   EMPTY SKY, EARTH BAKED HARD,
>   BROWN DUST STIRS ACROSS THE PLAIN.
>   WIND TURNS AROUND, BLOWS FROM THE EAST,
>   AND DOWN COMES THE SWEET SUMMER RAIN,
>   GREENING UP THE GRASS,
>   WASHING DOWN THE LEAVES,
>   SOAKING THROUGH THE EARTH ACROSS THE PLAIN.
>   EYES CLEAR OF DUST SEE A DIFFERENT LAND,
>   THE DRY EARTH DRINKS THE SUMMER RAIN, THE SUMMER
>   RAIN…
>   HEAR HOW IT SINGS IN THE HOT NEW YEAR

Anthony Weigh as Johnny and Genevieve Lemon as Peg in the 1997
Queensland Theatre Company production in Brisbane. (Photo: Paul Aurisch)

AS IT COURSES DOWN THE IRON ROOF AND OVERFLOWS
   THE GUTTER,
CALLS LIKE THE MAIL-TRAIN YOU STRAIN TO HEAR,
STIRS IN THE SHE-OAKS WHERE THE BULLFROGS MUTTER.
AND I'M STANDING IN THE RAIN,
DRINKING AS IT FALLS,
HAPPY THAT THE EARTH WILL LIVE AGAIN,
WIND FROM THE EAST STIRRING IN THE LEAVES,
AND DRY EARTH DRINKS THE SUMMER RAIN,
THE SUMMER RAIN.

JOHNNY: Two years I spent in the Western Desert. Our war, someone else's land. Back here now, it feels like someone else's show. I don't belong. Not to the troupe, not to a town. But I come here... I see what the rain does for you. And something else comes down with the rain. Something new for me. Something...

SINGS LIKE THE RAIN IN THE HOT NEW YEAR,
AS IT COURSES DOWN THE IRON ROOF AND OVERFLOWS
   THE GUTTER,
CALLS LIKE THE MAIL-TRAIN YOU STRAIN TO HEAR,
STIRS IN THE SHE-OAKS WHERE THE BULLFROGS MUTTER.
AS I SEE YOU IN THE RAIN, DRINKING AS IT FALLS,
HAPPY THAT THE EARTH WILL LIVE AGAIN;
WIND BLOWS WET, FEEL IT ON MY CHEEK,

PEG: WIND BLOWS WET, FEEL IT ON MY CHEEK,

PEG/JOHNNY: AND LOVE COMES DOWN LIKE SUMMER RAIN,
LOVE COMES DOWN LIKE SUMMER RAIN,
LIKE SUMMER RAIN.

They might be about to embrace. She breaks.

PEG: Goodnight.

She runs inside, leaving JOHNNY *alone in the dark street.*

END OF ACT ONE

ACT TWO

SCENE ONE

HAROLD *rehearses alone. He's startled to see* CATHY *watching in the shadows.*

HAROLD: Don't do that to a man! How long have you been watching?

CATHY: Ages. You talk to yourself. And you look that serious. When Clarrie and them do an act on New Year's Eve, they can hardly get through it for laughing.

HAROLD: But if it's your livelihood, you live or die by what you do. Do you understand that?

CATHY: But it's just mucking around, isn't it? Singing and dancing and telling jokes.

HAROLD: Plus the odd bit of magic.

He pulls a flower from behind her ear.

CATHY: How do you do that?

HAROLD: Trade secret.

Perhaps he does another small trick?

CATHY: When I come with you, you can show me— [all your secrets.]

HAROLD: Put that idea right out of your head, Cathy.

CATHY: Please.

HAROLD: Go on, run away before you get me in more strife. Every time you come near me, someone tries to run me out of town.

He goes back to his routine.

CATHY: We're safe as houses. I'm meant to be helping Auntie Reen with the New Year's Eve decorations, but she let me sneak down here.

HAROLD: There's nothing to see. Just a rehearsal.

CATHY: It's more fun than anything else going on round here. You're
bloody lucky, you know, Harold. You get paid to have fun.

HAROLD: Fun, she calls it. Fun!

CATHY: Well, it's not boring. It's different.

HAROLD: It's certainly that. A world of its own...
It's a world of leaky canvas, of mud and sodden guy-ropes,
A haven for desperates and misfits and crooks
Who walk a two-way tightrope from triumph to disaster,
Living on their nerve-ends, their lungs or their looks.
And the art of the profession, as we like to call our calling,
Is phoney smiles and hasty lies and midnight flits...
> AND THE SHOW GOES ON, THOUGH SINGAPORE IS
> FALLING,
> THROUGH PERITONITIS, CATARRH AND THE SQUITS,
> BUT...
> ONCE IN A BLUE MOON, IT'S WORTH ALL THE YACKER,
> THAT'S WHEN YOU TASTE THE LOVING CUP.
> YEAR AFTER YEAR THE GAME'S NOT WORTH A CRACKER,
> THEN THE MOON CHANGES COLOUR AND THE SKY
> LIGHTS UP.
> YES, NIGHTS ON END YOU'VE HALF A MIND TO CHUCK IT,
> STICK ON YOUR TOP HAT, GIVE IT ONE MORE CHANCE,
> 'CAUSE MAYBE TONIGHT YOU'LL CATCH THE LIGHTNING
> IN A BUCKET,
> IF THAT BLUE MOON'S SHINING AS YOU GO INTO YOUR
> DANCE.

CATHY: Still sounds like fun to me.

HAROLD: Then you've got a bloody funny idea of fun.
> IT'S A WORLD OF LUMPY MATTRESSES, AND BEDBUGS AND
> MOZZIES,
> RAILWAY REFRESHMENT ROOMS AND BROWN WINDSOR
> SOUP,
> GREASEPAINT RUNNING OFF YOU, STINKING SWEATY
> COSSIES,
> PAPER-THIN WALLS AND A BABY WITH CROUP;
> IT'S THE INGENUE WHO ROBS YOU, AND RUNS OFF WITH
> THE DRUMMER,

Donna Lee as Joy and Jonathan Biggins as Clarrie in the 1989 Sydney Theatre
Company production. *(Photo: Sandy Edwards, STC Archives)*

IT'S SMILING THROUGH THE SILENCE WHEN YOUR BEST
    JOKE DIED;
IT'S HAY AND HELL AND BOOLIGAL, AND BROKEN HILL
    IN SUMMER,
A HAND-CRANKED MERRY-GO-ROUND AT SIXPENCE A
    RIDE, BUT…
ONCE IN A BLUE MOON, IT'S WORTH ALL THE YACKER,
THAT'S WHEN YOU TASTE THE LOVING CUP.
YEAR AFTER YEAR THE GAME'S NOT WORTH A CRACKER
THEN THE MOON CHANGES COLOUR AND THE SKY
    LIGHTS UP.
YES, NIGHTS ON END YOU'VE HALF A MIND TO CHUCK IT,
STICK ON YOUR TOP HAT, GIVE IT ONE MORE CHANCE,
'CAUSE MAYBE TONIGHT YOU'LL CATCH THE LIGHTNING
    IN A BUCKET,
IF THAT BLUE MOON'S SHINING AS YOU GO INTO YOUR—

Dance break. RUBY *dresses him and joins him in a routine on stage
that night.*

RUBY/HAROLD: YES, NIGHTS ON END, YOU'VE HALF A MIND TO CHUCK
    IT,
    THEN COMES THE NIGHT YOU SEE THE MOON TURN BLUE;
    AND WHADDYA KNOW, YOU'VE CAUGHT THE LIGHTNING
    IN A BUCKET,
RUBY: FOR THAT BLUE MOON BEAMING
RUBY/HAROLD: SENDS THE MOONBEAMS STREAMING
    AND THE BRIGHT STAR GLEAMING IS YOU!
HAROLD: Thank you, ladies and gents. And now a musical drama of
    town and country life, in which my very own daughter, the lovely,
    leggy Joy Slocum is joined by your very own son, the lovely, leggy
    Clarrie Nugent.

    He brings on JOY *in 'rural' costume,* CLARRIE *as an old-style city
    slicker.*

CLARRIE: I'M A PLUSHY PITT STREET FARMER
    WITH CITY AIRS AND GRACES,
    EYEING A COUNTRY CHARMER
    AT THE GANG-GANG PICNIC RACES.

JOY: THIS JOKER FROM THE CITY
THINKS HE'LL HOLD A GIRL TO RANSOM;
CLARRIE: I'LL TELL HER SHE'S AWFULLY PRETTY—
JOY: I'LL TELL HIM HE'S TALL, DARK AND… SKINNY.
CLARRIE: HERE'S A DARK HANDSOME CHAPPY,
JOY: BIT OF A DILL—
CLARRIE: DRESSES EVER SO SNAPPY,
JOY: DRESSES TO KILL—
CLARRIE: SAYS HE'LL NEVER BE HAPPY,
JOY: NO, NOT UNTIL
JOY/CLARRIE: WE ARE WOOING, BILLING AND COOING.
JOY: A YOUNG CASANOVA,
CLARRIE: DASHING AND DROLL,
JOY: WHO IS LOOKING ME OVER,
CLARRIE: BODY AND SOUL,
JOY: WITH AN EYE OUT FOR CLOVER
WHERE WE CAN—
CLARRIE: STROLL!
JOY: IN THE CLOVER,
CLARRIE: SWEET AS PAVLOVA.
JOY: I KNOW A GIRL SHOULD CUT AND RUN,
BUT CUT AND RUN MEANS CUT THE FUN,
I'LL SIT AND SMILE AND CHECK HIS STYLE.
CLARRIE: MY JOY, MY LIFE, MY DREAM OF BLISS…
JOY: AW, CUT THE CACKLE, TRY A KISS.
CLARRIE: A KISS?
JOY: LIKE THIS!
CLARRIE: GOD GAVE US EYES TO GAZE, SOULS TO FUSE,
HEARTS TO BLAZE—
JOY: AND LIPS TO USE!

She grabs him and smooches him.

JOY/CLARRIE: HERE'S A DARK HANDSOME CHAPPY, FEELING A FLUSH,
GETTING SOGGY AND SAPPY, TURNING TO MUSH,
JOY: COME ON BOY, MAKE IT SNAPPY!

She produces a veil and bouquet.

CLARRIE: HEY WHAT'S THE RUSH?

JOY: QUICK, THE VICAR, I'VE CAUGHT A CITY SLICKER!

JOY/CLARRIE: AND SOON THE RING IS PICKED OUT,
              THE LITTLE CHURCH IS TRICKED OUT,
              THE STEEPLE BELLS ARE RINGING,
              THE CHOIR'S SWEETLY SINGING: A-MEN!
              AND WHEN A DARK, HANDSOME CHAPPIE,
              LEARNS TO CHANGE A NAPPY,
              A MAMMY AND PAPPY YOU'LL SEE:
              HOW HAPPY WE'LL BE!

They dance off. HAROLD *begins his magic act.* RUBY *finds* BARRY *outside the hall.*

RUBY: There are seats inside, you know.

BARRY: I'm happy here.

RUBY: It's a good turnout in there. Best we've had in months. You'd enjoy yourself. But you've made your stand, haven't you? So you'll stop out here in the wet, with your ear pressed up against the back wall. You're a real sad sack, you know. Come on, Barry! Bite back.

BARRY: Mrs Slocum, I'm not dirty on you.

RUBY: You're dirty on the whole world.

BARRY: You're not too bloody cheerful yourself. Look, Mrs Slocum—

RUBY: It's Ruby. You know the woman in the good book whose price is above rubies? I'm the one whose price is below hers. Well below. One thing I'd like to know about you…

BARRY: I ought to be getting back to the pub.

RUBY: What for? No one's drinking, they're all in here. Tell Ruby, has there been anyone in your life since Nancy?

Silence. Then he shakes his head.

Christ. Did you tie a knot in it? Oh, I've shocked him.

BARRY: I don't shock that easy. I've never seen anyone that could come up to her.

RUBY: Hadn't you better start looking? We're into the second show of the night, Barry. We haven't got that much time to waste.

BARRY: Then why do you stick with Slocum?

RUBY: Good question.

BARRY: Plenty of blokes would think themselves lucky to hook up with someone like—not that I'm trying to put the hard word on you.

RUBY: Maybe I wish you were.

He stares at her, then grins.

Wouldn't be the end of the world. We're only human. We all need our backs scratched on a regular basis.

BARRY: But it's hard to find a free pair of hands in a small town.

He starts to chuckle.

RUBY: Hard enough in a big town. Unless you've got Harold's knack. Or do I mean Harold's knackers?

RENIE *comes out and sees them laughing together.*

RENIE: Mrs Slocum, they want you on the stage.

RUBY *passes her.* RENIE *glares at* BARRY. *He goes.* HAROLD *finishes the trick, producing a delighted* CATHY *instead of* JOY. *Applause.*

HAROLD: Now, friends, we end tonight's show with the golden tones of the pride of the 2nd/24th Battalion, Corporal John Slocum.

JOHNNY *comes on in uniform.*

JOHNNY: THE SUNBURST ON MY BADGE, THE BUCKLE ON MY BELT,
HAVE JUST HAD THEIR FINAL SHINE.
THE SHIP HAS COME INTO PORT,
THE BAND IS ON THE DOCK,
THERE'S A TINGLE RUNNING DOWN MY SPINE.
AND AS SOON AS THE GANGPLANK'S DOWN,
WE START THE MARCH THROUGH TOWN.
AND AT THE END OF THE PARADE THERE'LL BE SOMEONE,
AT THE END OF THE PARADE THERE SHE'LL BE,
STANDING STRAIGHT AND PROUD, WAVING THROUGH THE CROWD,
HANDS REACHING OUT TO ME.
THE LIGHT IN HER EYES WILL BE SHINING,
THAT LIGHT I KNEW WOULD NEVER FADE;
AND TODAY WILL BE WORTH THE WAITING,
FOR SHE'S WAITING AT THE END OF THE PARADE.

HAROLD, JOY *and* RUBY *join him.*

TROUPE: AND AT THE END OF THE PARADE THERE'LL BE SOMEONE,
AT THE END OF THE PARADE THERE SHE'LL BE,
STANDING STRAIGHT AND PROUD, WAVING THROUGH
   THE CROWD,
HANDS REACHING OUT TO ME.
THE LIGHT IN HER EYES WILL BE SHINING,
THAT LIGHT I KNEW WOULD NEVER EVER FADE;
AND TODAY WILL BE WORTH THE WAITING,
FOR SHE'S WAITING AT THE END OF THE PARADE.

Patriotic tableau. Applause. RENIE *and* CATHY *clap in the wings.* HAROLD *starts a curtain speech but* MAISIE *comes onto the stage with* RED *and* CLARRIE *and other* TOWNSPEOPLE.

MAISIE: What a night this has been for Turna! Red?

RED: It was a tip-top show. Yes, tip-top. Absolutely tip-top.

LORNA: It was even better than Red doing 'Clancy of the Overflow', and that's saying something.

RED: Break it down, Lorn. Well, thanks from Turna. It was… tip-top. Over to you, Maise.

MAISIE: Now, Harold, Ruby, John, Joy, the town would like to invite you all to our show.

HAROLD: Oh, you do a show?

CLARRIE: She means New Year's Eve, mate. Our mob will all turn out in their gladrags. And your mob'll be the guests of honour.

RUBY: But we'll be gone by then.

MAISIE: The Slocum family is not going anywhere before the New Year. Not after the joy you've given us tonight.

CLARRIE *winks at* JOY.

CLARRIE: No pun intended.

MAISIE: We'll see the New Year in together.

HAROLD: Yes, we will, thank you. Won't we, kids?

JOY *and* JOHNNY *agree.*

CLARRIE: Whacko. Now it's back to the Shamrock. And drinks are on me!

He puts an arm around JOY. RED *presses a bag of takings into* HAROLD's *hand. All head off.* RUBY *intercepts* HAROLD.

RUBY: Did we do okay?

He jingles the bag.

I mean the show. God, four of us out there doing the work of fourteen! Was it okay?

HAROLD: You heard the man, a tip-top night. Come on.

RUBY: Harold, have I done all right by you?

HAROLD: You're a pro, Ruby. A lovely mover, nice timing—

RUBY: I don't mean the show. I could have left you on Christmas Eve. But you wanted to come here, and I came. Now I want to go. The creek's dropping, we could get out tomorrow. Please, Hallie.

HAROLD: We just accepted an invitation to—

RUBY: You accepted. For all of us.

HAROLD: Johnny and Joycie looked thrilled.

RUBY: I can see why Joy and Johnny want to stick around. But what's here for you, Harold?

HAROLD: I don't know. Yes, I do. I felt it tonight, a touch of the old magic. It felt like my first show…

RUBY: It felt like my last.

HAROLD: … the first time I knew who I was. [*He hasn't heard her. He sheds his cloak.*] Come on, darl. We've earned ourselves a free drink.

RUBY: You go. I have to change.

He nods, gives her the cloak, then goes with the money.

No, Harold. You change. Or I have to go.

YOU WITH THE MAGIC WAND,
YES, YOU WITH THE CLOAK,
MY ABRACADABRA MAN.
I LOVE EVERY TRICK,
I'D SAY I'M YOUR GREATEST FAN,
BUT YOU'VE BEEN A MAN OF MYSTERY
SINCE THE ACT BEGAN.
ONE WAVE OF YOUR MAGIC WAND,
A FLICK OF YOUR CLOAK

AND I WAS BENEATH YOUR SPELL,
THEN YOU DISAPPEARED,
BUT HOW, I COULD NEVER TELL,
SO I LOST THAT MAGIC MAN
I THOUGHT I KNEW SO WELL.
LONG YEARS I WAITED
WHERE WERE YOU? SILLY ME,
MEANT TO SAY: WHERE WERE WE?
LONG, LONG YEARS I WAITED,
AFRAID TO FACE THE FACT
I'VE NEVER EVER CRACKED
YOUR DISAPPEARING ACT.
NOW HE'S GONE WITH HIS MAGIC WAND,
THE BLOKE IN THE CLOAK
HAS VANISHED IN SMOKE, MY MANDRAKE,
LEAVING ME TO PONDER,
PONDER WHERE THE CLOAK AND WAND ARE,
WHERE IS MY ABRACADABRA MAN?

SCENE TWO

PEG and MICK serve behind the bar. All the TOWN is there. MAISIE, RENIE, LORNA, RED and CLARRIE salute JOY, HAROLD, RUBY and JOHNNY. CATHY follows. BARRY comes from upstairs.

BARRY: Cathy's not in her room. [He sees CATHY.] You gave me your word. Get upstairs.

CLARRIE: Barry, we asked her to help backstage. It was our fault.

RENIE: It was no one's fault. It was right and proper. It made her part of the show.

BARRY: Made her break her word. The creek's down below the bridge. This crowd are moving on tomorrow.

MAISIE: We've asked them to stay for the dance, son.

LORNA: There'll never be a New Year's Eve like this one, Dad, and we want them here.

BARRY: And who's we, Lorna?

RENIE: Oh, for God's sake! If Nancy was here—

BARRY: You only got one bloody thing to say? Like some old parrot?

PEG: Dad!

RENIE: You apologise for that.

PEG: Shut up, the both of you. Listen to me, Dad. Cathy broke her word, but you had no right to ask it of her. She's not a kid no more, and she needs—

BARRY: I don't want to talk about Cathy.

PEG: Then talk about me. I've held this place together for you for seven years, and I'm putting in my bill. I want us to forget and forgive and have our New Year's Eve together. That means all of us, Cath included. Come the New Year, we'll say our goodbyes, and these people will get on their way. But in the meantime I want them here. They're not strangers no more. They're part of us, at least till New Year's Day. Fair enough?

BARRY: Fair enough.

He goes. All leave PEG *to clean up with* MICK.

MICK: Big speech. Longest I've ever heard you talk. 'They're not strangers no more.'

PEG: I'm glad you agree.

MICK: I don't. I'm just wondering what you meant.

PEG: What I said.

MICK: I know what's going on, Peg.

PEG: Do you? You're one up on me, then.

MICK: I want you to promise me—

PEG: I can't promise nothing.

MICK: Don't make a laughing stock of me. That's all I'm asking.

PEG: That's all you're asking?

Silence.

Mick, I wish you'd been at that show. Would have been good to see you crack a smile.

MICK: I'll smile when there's something worth smiling about.

He goes. She cleans up. JOHNNY *appears.*

PEG: Keep your distance. I'm calling a halt to this.

JOHNNY: Before anything's even started?

PEG: Something did start. And now I'm stopping it.

JOHNNY: You can't. And you know why. We're in each other's heads.

PEG: Sounds like an old line to me.

JOHNNY: I started out slinging you the old lines, but now it's gone way beyond that. I don't know what to say, 'cause I've never met anyone like you. You're one of a kind. That's why you're in my head... no, in my heart. You're in my heart, Peg, and that's the truth.

PEG: Your truth. At the end of the day you're a showie. You see the world in bright colours, all dancing and music and romance. I watched you up there tonight in your nice clean uniform, singing like a bird. 'At the end of the parade there'll be someone...' You think it was like that for the people that went through it?

JOHNNY: I went through it. Four years of it. I'd like to have had someone waiting for me, someone like—

PEG: At least you could walk off the boat. Mick didn't come marching down no gangplank. He copped a shell in Borneo. They carried him off on a stretcher.

JOHNNY: Poor bugger.

PEG: He was lucky. His best mate was blown to smithereens in front of his eyes. My Uncle Col McKenna went the same way. That's the way things happen in real life. This thing isn't real. You're a library book, Johnny. In a couple of days I'll have to hand you back, and the van will drive away.

JOHNNY: What the hell are you talking about!

PEG: Cavanagh's Travelling Library.

> JUST FOUR TIMES A YEAR ON THE SHAMROCK VERANDAH,
> I'D WAIT FOR THE VAN
> THAT BROUGHT ME MY DREAMS:
> STORIES OF GRAND AND IMPOSSIBLE THINGS,
> PRINCES AND BEGGARMAIDS, DRAGONS AND KINGS,
> EACH ONE I LOVED,
> BUT THERE'S ONE THAT FILLED MY DREAMS;
> THE DREAMS OF NANCY'S DAUGHTER,
> THE DREAMS OF PEGGY DOYLE...

THERE'S A DARK, HANDSOME STRANGER
COMES MY WAY IN THE MOONLIGHT,
AS IT GLOWS ON THE FOUNTAIN ACROSS THE LAWN.
I'LL COME DOWN FROM MY WINDOW
AND I'LL CLIMB ON HIS CHARGER,
AND WE'LL RIDE OFF IN GLORY INTO THE DAWN.
I LOVED THAT STORY ON THE PAGE
UNTIL I PASSED THE READING AGE,
AT SEVENTEEN, I CLOSED THE BOOK.
NOW TEN YEARS ON, THE STRANGER'S HERE,
HIS EYES ON MINE AS HE COMES NEAR;
I DARE NOT LOOK:
BUT HOPE THE STRANGER WILL RIDE AWAY,
RIDE AWAY BY BREAK OF DAY...
THOUGH THE MOON'S ON THE FOUNTAIN,
AND THE STRANGER IS HANDSOME,
AND HIS CHARGER CAN BEAR US TO PARTS UNKNOWN,
WE WON'T RIDE OFF IN GLORY—
THAT ENDS SOMEONE ELSE'S STORY...
STRANGER, RIDE ON ALONE.

JOHNNY: That doesn't have to be the story, not this time.

PEG: Yes, it has to be. Ride on, Johnny. I've got a life here.

JOHNNY: The life you want?

PEG: Want isn't in it. I've got a husband.

JOHNNY: Who'll be unhappy, with you or without you. That's pity, not love. It'll eat you both up. I want to take you with me, Peg. Anywhere you want. But I need the word from you. Come outside. The rain's let up. We could walk down to the creek.

PEG: And see the moon on the water? No, I need to do some thinking. On my own. Off you go. Please. Go on.

JOHNNY: Okay. But either way... you owe me one dance on New Year's Eve. One dance. Something to remember you by, Peggy. Not that I'll need a reminder. You're here, I told you. For as long as you like. Even longer.

She nods. He goes. She watches him move into the street. Each is alone. Each sings against the other.

PEG: THOUGH THE MOON'S ON THE FOUNTAIN,
   AND THE STRANGER IS HANDSOME,
   AND HIS CHARGER CAN BEAR US TO PARTS UNKNOWN,
   WE WON'T RIDE OFF IN GLORY
   THAT ENDS SOMEONE ELSE'S STORY
   STRANGER, RIDE ON ALONE.

JOHNNY: AT THE END OF THE PARADE THERE'LL BE SOMEONE,
   AT THE END OF THE PARADE, THERE SHE'LL BE.
   I KNOW SHE'LL BE.
   I KNOW THE FACE I'LL SEE THERE,
   I KNOW THAT SHE WILL BE THERE,
   AT THE END OF THE PARADE.

She turns out the lights.

SCENE THREE

Dusk on New Year's Eve. CLARRIE, MICK *and* RED *string up lanterns.* RUBY *and* JOY *make decorations.*

RUBY: Clarrie Nugent. Now I've heard everything.

JOY: He told me I'm the one for him.

RUBY: Joycie, so did the Dalgety's man in Mudgee.

JOY: Yes, but Clarrie's single.

RUBY: Granted.

JOY: And I think I might love him.

RUBY: Then go for your life. Here. [*She slips off her earrings.*] I wore these the night your father proposed.

JOY: Thanks.

RUBY: And if they do you any good, sling them back my way. How will Clarrie cope with being on the road?

JOY: He won't have to.

RUBY: You're going to give up the business?

JOY: Too right. I'm going to have four kids and a garden and teach ballroom dancing in the School of Arts. When Mum left Harold I thought she was giving up on life. Now I know what she was after, a chance to sit and breathe. But I'll miss you, Rube.

RUBY: Now, how do we break the news to Harold?

JOY: Hold your horses, I got to break it to Clarrie first.

In the hotel, HAROLD *dresses for the night.*

HAROLD: 1946, son, a whole new story. I'll write you some new patter—

JOHNNY: Dad, it isn't the show. It's me that doesn't fit. Not any more.

HAROLD: You've had another offer.

JOHNNY: Not quite. Listen to me—

HAROLD: Is it the money?

JOHNNY: Christ, no, or I would have shot through years ago. I need to move on.

HAROLD: You want to work legit. I could run you up some dramatic monologues—

JOHNNY: Will you listen, just once! You've never listened, except for your next cue.

HAROLD: I've done my best for you, my boy.

JOHNNY: I was never a boy, Dad.

HAROLD: When your mother dumped me, you had your choice. You could have gone with her, Johnny. But you stayed with Dad.

JOHNNY: Because I was a pro, even at twelve. I couldn't let you down. Anyway, what other kind of life did I know?

HAROLD: What other kind do you know now? All right, you've seen some action, and I'm proud of you. But you'll get back into swing with us, Johnny-cake.

JOHNNY: No, Dad! No more Johnny-cake. And no more trouping.

HAROLD: You see how you feel tomorrow. It's a tough world out there on your own.

He goes.

JOHNNY: Who says I'm going to be on my own?

PEG *wears a yellow dress which* LORNA *has just finished.* CATHY *watches.*

CATHY: Pretty material. What do you call it?

LORNA: Georgette.

PEG: Renie had it tucked away. She gave it to me for Christmas. I reckon tonight's the night for this colour. I'm wearing Mumma's earrings as well.

LORNA: You wouldn't do better out of the DJ's catalogue.

PEG: Lorna, you're a wonder-worker. Look at the way it moves, Cath! I want to show this to Renie.

   She runs out.

CATHY: It's not Renie she wants to show.

   LORNA *shushes* CATHY *and takes the baby away.* PEG *runs into* BARRY *on the verandah.*

BARRY: Nancy...

    THERE'S A LAUGHING WOMAN AT A NEW YEAR DANCE, SHE WEARS A YELLOW DRESS...

I'm sorry...

PEG: Eh?

BARRY: Sorry... I never seen you in that colour before.

PEG: No. I think it suits me, though. Don't you?

BARRY: Peggy... you do know what you're doing?

PEG: I'm getting ready for tonight, Dad.

   She goes towards Renie's place.

BARRY: I MET THE WOMAN UNDERNEATH THE CASUARINA TREE;
    SHE WORE A DRESS OF YELLOW LAWN, A SHAWL OF FILIGREE.
    HER HAIR WAS BURNISHED COPPER, HER EYES WERE LIKE THE SEA;
    THE BREEZE STIRRED IN THE HORSE-TAILS OF THE CASUARINA TREE...
    SHE-OAK BY THE RIVERBANK SIGHING, LOVER COME CLOSE TO ME.
    WE LAY TOGETHER UNDERNEATH THE CASUARINA TREE;
    SHE LOOSED HER HAIR AND SPREAD HER SHAWL,
    AND GAVE HERSELF TO ME.
    THE RIVER RAN BESIDE US, AND FLOWED ON TO THE SEA;
    ABOVE US WERE THE HEAVENS AND THE CASUARINA TREE...
    SHE-OAK BY THE RIVERBANK SIGHING, LOVER COME CLOSE TO ME.
    THE DAWN CAME AS WE LAY BENEATH THE CASUARINA TREE.

I SAW THOSE BLUE EYES OPEN, FAR DEEPER THAN THE SEA;
SHE SAID, 'I'M YOURS FOREVER, YOUR LOVER WILL I BE.'
OUR LOVE WAS SEALED THAT NIGHT BENEATH THE
    CASUARINA TREE.
SHE-OAK BY THE RIVERBANK SIGHING, LOVER STAY CLOSE
    TO ME.
NOW THE RIVER RUNS AGAIN BESIDE THE CASUARINA
    TREE;
THERE'S ONE I'LL LOVE FOREVER, BUT NEVERMORE WILL
    SEE;
TONIGHT I'LL BEG FORGIVENESS, THAT ONCE SHE BEGGED
    OF ME,
THE WOMAN DRESSED IN YELLOW 'NEATH THE
    CASUARINA TREE...
SHE-OAK BY THE RIVERBANK SIGHING, LOVER COME
    CLOSE TO ME.

SCENE FOUR

New Year's dance. All mingle. JOHNNY *teaches* CATHY *to polka.* MAISIE
claps her hands.

MAISIE: Friends, it's getting dangerously close to 1946. Take your
partners, please. We have only one rule. No wives and husbands
dancing till after midnight! Let's raise the dust.

RED: No dust this year, Maise.

MAISIE: Then we'll raise the mud, Red, and dance the New Year in.

ALL: TAKE THE YEAR AND DRUM IT OUT,
           TAKE THE YEAR AND DRUM IT OUT,
           TAKE THE YEAR AND DRUM IT OUT, OLD YEAR.
           NEW YEAR'S EVE IN TURNAROUND CREEK IS HERE.
           GREET THE YEAR AND RING IT IN,
           GREET THE YEAR AND RING IT IN,
           GREET THE YEAR AND RING IT IN, NEW YEAR.
           NEW YEAR'S EVE IN TURNAROUND CREEK IS HERE.
           YES, THE YEAR WE LIVED CAN DIE NOW,

PASS AWAY WITH A SIGH NOW,
THE NEW YEAR IS DUE HERE AND COMING.
SO DRUM OUT THE OLD YEAR,
DANCE IN THE COMING YEAR,
IT'S COMING, IT'S HUMMING,
SO DRUM IT IN, DRUM IT IN!
OLD YEAR GOING, DRUM IT OUT, OLD YEAR! /
NEW YEAR COMING, RING IT IN, NEW YEAR!
OLD YEAR GONE AND TURNAROUND'S COME THROUGH,
NEW YEAR COME AND TURNAROUND'S COME TO,
NEW YEAR'S EVE AND TURNAROUND CREEK'S STILL HERE!

Dance break.

MAISIE: It's almost midnight.

ALL: IT'S COMING, SO DRUM IT IN, DRUM IT IN!

MEN: OLD YEAR GOING, DRUM IT OUT, OLD YEAR

WOMEN: NEW YEAR COMING, RING IT IN, NEW YEAR…

ALL: OLD YEAR GONE AND TURNAROUND'S COME THROUGH,
NEW YEAR COME AND TURNAROUND'S COME TO,
NEW YEAR'S EVE AND TURNAROUND CREEK'S STILL HERE!
HAPPY NEW YEAR!

MAISIE: Mr and Mrs Slocum, by tradition the waltz comes now, so the couples can start the New Year in each other's arms. As our guests of honour, you'll lead off for us.

She brings HAROLD *and* RUBY *together. They waltz.* MICK *stands by* PEG. LORNA *and* RED *take the floor.* CLARRIE *partners* JOY. BARRY *approaches* RENIE.

BARRY: You going to give me this one?

RENIE: Go and dance with that Ruby, if you're so stuck on her.

BARRY shrugs and cuts in on HAROLD. RUBY dances with him. HAROLD dances with MAISIE. JOHNNY approaches PEG. MICK watches.

RUBY: Renie gave you the bum's rush?

BARRY: Her and me had a barney the other night. I tried to make it up, but—

RUBY: Try again. You miss your moment tonight, it might never come round again.

BARRY: She's ignoring me—

RUBY: She hasn't taken her eyes off you all night. I'd say it's you been ignoring her, and for years, eh? Go on, make a fuss of her.

BARRY: One more turn, Ruby. I'm enjoying this.

RUBY: She's not. Anyway, one more turn and I might be too hot and bothered to let you go. Scram.

She spins him towards RENIE, *and disengages* CLARRIE *from* JOY. LORNA *passes* RED *to* JOY.

BARRY: Renie? Come on...

RENIE: Mr Slocum? Maisie, I'm cutting in.

She moves to dance with HAROLD. MICK *intercepts* PEG *and* JOHNNY *as they pass him, and breaks them up.*

MICK: One dance, you said.

PEG: I haven't heard the music finish.

MICK: This is finished.

PEG: Mick, give it a rest. People are staring...

MICK: Like they been for days. You've made us a laughing-stock in front of the whole town...

He collars JOHNNY, *who squares up to him.*

JOHNNY: That's all that matters?

BARRY approaches.

What about Peg's feelings? Do they ever matter to you?

PEG: Stay out of this, Dad.

BARRY: I got one thing to say—

PEG: Don't.

BARRY: Leave them be, Mick.

He draws MICK *away.*

MICK: If that had been anyone else but you, Barry...

BARRY: You and me need to have a few words.

CATHY and HAROLD are dancing.

MICK: Aren't you going to put a stop to that first?

BARRY: No, son.

The DANCERS *disappear. The waltz dies.*

MICK: Like father, like son. They're a couple of mug lairs.

BARRY: And what are we?

MICK: Eh?

BARRY: I know what I am, son. A blind fool. When I saw Peggy in that dress, it hit me like a sledge-hammer, the things I never said to Nance. Oh, you speak your heart in the moonlight when you're both young and eager. But then you settle down. You shut down. You get caught up in your own troubles. You ignore this woman, this beautiful woman. Then Slocum's mob roll in…

MICK: Why are you telling me this, Barry!

BARRY: You've had your own troubles. Big ones. But Peg's been beside you every step of the way.

MICK: I treat her all right, don't I? What do I do wrong?

BARRY: You drive into Gidgeree once a fortnight. Ever take her with you? Ever bring her back a little something nice, chocolates or scent? Or a book? She's always been a reader.

MICK: She's got the Travelling Library.

BARRY: Cavanagh's haven't been round once since you got home. Did you notice her dress tonight? Ever seen her in that colour before?

MICK: Where do you reckon she'll be?

BARRY: I dunno. By the creek? I reckon that's where most people will be heading tonight.

MICK: What do I do? Go and find her?

BARRY: Up to you. You know what they say, though. You miss your moment, it might never come round again.

He goes.

MICK: TONIGHT THE CREEK IS BRIMMING BY THE CASUARINA TREE;

THERE'S MOONLIGHT ON THE WATER AS IT FLOWS DOWN TO THE SEA.

TONIGHT AGAIN I'LL FIND HER, WHERE IS SHE, WHERE IS SHE?

THE WOMAN DRESSED IN YELLOW 'NEATH THE CASUARINA TREE…

Peggy…

He goes off into the night.

SCENE FIVE

Outside. Early hours of New Year's Day. CLARRIE *and* JOY *are arm-in-arm. He carries something over one arm.*

JOY: WATCH THE PUDDLES...
What happened to the street, Clarrie? I don't see the War Memorial. Where are we going?

CLARRIE: Down by the creek, soft summer breeze, moon on the water, the full bit. And if you squint hard enough I could easy turn into Tyrone Power.

JOY: It'll be a bit damp underfoot, won't it?

CLARRIE: What do you know, I brought this groundsheet. Gift of a grateful nation to Lance Corporal Clarrie Nugent.

They go as MAISIE *pursues* RENIE.

RENIE: No, Maise. I've had this town.

MAISIE: You mean you've had Barry Doyle.

RENIE: I'm sick of the bloody mention of his name. I'm packing up, Maise. I'll start again somewhere else.

MAISIE: Well, you're a mature woman, you know your own mind. If you're happy to go without making your peace with Barry—

RENIE: Barry Doyle. I'm sick of the bloody mention of his name. Did you see him tonight? Couldn't keep his hands off Ruby Slocum. He was drooling that much it was running down his chin.

MAISIE: You had your hands full with Harold.

RENIE: I was feeling friendly.

MAISIE: I'll say. Frisky as a poddy calf.

RENIE: I wasn't! Was I?

She sees RUBY *approaching.*

I'm off.

RUBY: No you're not.

RENIE: In the morning I'll be off on the train to freedom.

She hurries away.

RUBY: Renie! Oh, God. I tell you, Miss Trengrove, this place wasn't built for high heels.

She pursues RENIE. JOHNNY *is alone with* PEG.

JOHNNY: All we've done is talk about Mick.

PEG: You did ask.

JOHNNY: When?

PEG: That first night, remember?

JOHNNY: I asked other questions. Your favourite smell...

PEG: The bush after rain.

JOHNNY: What's in this locket...

PEG: What do you think? Mum's picture.

JOHNNY: Last question. What about us?

PEG: You tell me.

JOHNNY: Okay. We'll go away together. No more Turna, no more troupe. Something new for both of us.

PEG: I don't know if I can do that.

JOHNNY: I know one thing. You got to say goodbye to someone in the morning.

PEG: I can't think about the morning.

She kisses him.

Come on. The swimming hole's full up again. We better see it while it's here to be seen.

They go. RUBY *pursues* RENIE.

RENIE: All right, I believe you. Anyway, Barry bloody Doyle is nothing to me. Less than nothing.

RUBY: Dust beneath your feet. You're heading out. A free woman.

RENIE: Free of Barry bloody Doyle, at any rate. I don't know why us ladies have to be forever talking about blokes. But Barry bloody Doyle—

RUBY: Three times in thirty seconds. Barry bloody Doyle. What about him? Tell Ruby. Get it out, darl. Just like a splinter.

RENIE: Well, Ruby... No, there's nothing to tell. He's a dead-set mongrel, that's all.

RUBY: Renie, they all are.

RENIE: No! My Col wasn't.

Geraldine Turner (left) as Ruby and Gael Ballantyne as Renie in the 1997
Queesland Theatre Company production in Brisbane. (Photo: Rob MacColl)

RUBY: Then I wish I'd known him. He would have been the one exception to Ruby's universal rule.

>FROM MISTER CHIFLEY DOWNWARDS TO THE LOWEST COPPER'S NARK,
>
>EVERY MAN'S A CROCK, A CROOK, A CON,
>
>FROM MO McCACKIE UPWARDS TO...

RENIE: THE MAN FROM IRONBARK,

RUBY: AND MAYBE EVEN... YES, THE MIGHTY DON.

RENIE: Then why are we out here fretting while they're in there asleep? Why don't we have the mongrels put down?

RUBY: Why?

>THAT OLD LINE THEY SOLD US, AND TOLD US TO HOLD US:
>
>A MAN IS A WOMAN'S FATE—

RENIE: WHAT A FATE!

RUBY: TO COSSET AND PAMPER,

RENIE: PUT JAM ON HIS DAMPER, WHILE HE SITS THERE ON HIS—

RUBY: DATE.

>AND SOON AS THE BASTARD HAS GOT YOU LORD AND MASTERED,
>
>HE'LL COOK UP A LURK AND TRY IT ON.

RENIE: SO DUMP HIM!

RUBY: DUMP HIM? NO, SHAKE HIM UP AND THUMP HIM—
YOU MIGHT MISS THE MONGREL WHEN HE'S GONE.

RENIE: Miss him? I wouldn't have Barry bloody Doyle if you paid me.

RUBY: Still, you listen to Ruby and you'll learn something for next time.

>THERE'S NO POINT IN MOPING, OR COPING, OR HOPING
>
>THE MONGREL WILL KNOW HE'S DONE YOU WRONG.
>
>SO DON'T HAVE THE VAPOURS, HOLD THE WALKING PAPERS,
>
>HAVE A DECENT BARNEY AND YOU'LL...

RUBY/RENIE: SING LOVE'S OLD SWEET SONG.

RENIE: AND HOW DOES THAT SONG GO?

RUBY/RENIE: EVERY MAN'S A DRONGO,

RUBY: BUT ONE OR TWO ARE WORTH THE KEEPING ON;

RENIE: SO HAVE A DING-DONG, A DUST-UP,

RUBY: BUT NEVER EVER BUST UP,
            YOU MIGHT MISS THE MONGREL WHEN HE'S GONE.

RENIE: WELL, MAYBE…

RUBY/RENIE: WE MIGHT MISS THE MONGREL WHEN HE'S GONE.
            NOT THAT WE'D MISS—

RENIE: THE SULKING,

RUBY: THE SKULKING,

RENIE: THE GREYHOUND PUP HE HAD TO BUY;

RUBY: THE BAY RUM THAT LINGERS,

RENIE: THE NICOTINE FINGERS,

RUBY: THE LIPPY ON HIS HANKIE…

RUBY/RENIE: AND WONDERS WHY YOU'RE CRANKY!

RUBY/RENIE: NOT THAT WE'D MISS

RENIE: THE BLACK DAYS,

RUBY: THE SLACK DAYS,
            THE LUMINOUS NUDE UPON HIS TIE;

RENIE: 'WAKE UP, IT'S THE KID, LOVE.'

RUBY: 'LEND US A QUID, LOVE?'

RUBY/RENIE: THE CALLS TO THE BOOKIE—
            WE MIGHT MISS THE NOOKY.
            YES, IT'S AS PLAIN AS THE NOSES ON A MAN'S TWO FACES:
            THE MOMENT YOU START YOUR BIG ROMANCE,
            EVERY MOTHER'S SON AROUND WILL GIVE YOU THE
                RUNAROUND,
            ONCE YOU GIVE HIM HALF A CHANCE.

RENIE: SO TRAIN HIM,

RUBY: RESTRAIN HIM,

RUBY/RENIE: BUT CAREFUL NOT TO BRAIN HIM,
            HE WON'T BE MUCH USE WITHOUT A HEAD.

RENIE: AND AFTER YOU'VE DECKED HIM?

RUBY: BETTER RESURRECT HIM:

RUBY/RENIE: YOU MIGHT MISS THE MONGREL WHEN HE'S DEAD…
            AND GONE,
            YOU MIGHT MISS HIM WHEN HE'S…

RUBY: Barry Doyle or Pat Malone?
  Better the devil you've always known…
RUBY/RENIE: YOU MIGHT MISS HIM WHEN HE'S…
RENIE: Rube and Harold, two for the show?
  Better the devil you think you know…
RUBY/RENIE: YOU MIGHT MISS HIM WHEN HE'S GONE!

  They shake hands and go. BARRY *pursues* HAROLD.

BARRY: No, Harold. You got a story to finish.
HAROLD: If I tell you you'll only thump me again.
BARRY: Once was enough. Come on. The truth.
HAROLD: That New Year's Eve, out here in the moonlight, in the wet grass… I asked her to come away with me.
BARRY: And what did she say?

  Silence. Then HAROLD *shakes his head.*

  Why was she out here, then?
HAROLD: She needed company, a bit of sweet talk, even. But it was only you she loved.
BARRY: I loved her. Only I never told her. I'm sorry. I'm very sorry.
HAROLD: Don't apologise to me, mate.
BARRY: I'm talking to Nancy. I'm sorry for a lot of things, darling. And I'm sorry you're gone without hearing this.
HAROLD: When did she go?
BARRY: The night she had Cathy.
HAROLD: Cathy's a good kid. They're all good girls, the three of them.
BARRY: Cathy's different. She's…
HAROLD: She's young, Barry, she's restless.
BARRY: She's yours.
HAROLD: Oh, mate. Mine? Cathy's mine. I'm sorry.
BARRY: Don't apologise to me, mate.
HAROLD: I'm talking to Nancy. My kid. Is that why you're so hard on her?
BARRY: I might have been blaming her, for things that aren't her fault. Or I might be scared to let her go.
HAROLD: Because she's the last of Nancy?

  RUBY *emerges from the shadows.*

RUBY: The last of Nancy. Haven't you buried her yet? Boys, I'll give it to you straight. A dead woman can't keep you warm in bed. I'd go for the here and now. Down by the War Memorial there's a living woman, name of Renie McKenna. She's no Nancy, who could be? But she's got a good heart and lovely eyes. Why don't you go and take a look in those eyes? Off you go.

BARRY: Now?

RUBY: Now or never. It's all in the timing. Ask Harold. Did you track him down yet, darl? That fella you came back to find? Get a wriggle on. You've only got till morning. Same as Barry.

    She goes.

BARRY: That's a good woman. Here and now, she said. Can you face that?

HAROLD: Can you? I've got some memories to bury first.

    THAT MORNING—

BARRY: THAT MORNING—

HAROLD/BARRY: ON A HOTEL VERANDAH,

BARRY: HAIR LOOSE AND FLOWING,

HAROLD: BOUND IN A COIL,

BARRY: LOOKING FOR WORK WITH A SISTER IN TOW,

HAROLD: EYES THAT LIT UP WHEN I PROMISED A SHOW,

BARRY: EYES THAT REFLECTED THE MORNING,

HAROLD: THAT MORNING…

HAROLD/BARRY: THOSE EYES…

BARRY: THE EYES OF NANCY KEENAN,

HAROLD: THE EYES OF NANCY DOYLE.

HAROLD/BARRY: OTHER MORNINGS HAVE BROKEN,
        OTHER SUNS, OTHER SKIES,
        OTHER DAYS BY THE THOUSANDS,
        CLOSE THOSE EYES.
        LET THE NIGHT HAVE ITS PASSING,
        LET THE DAWN LIGHT THE SKIES,
        BUT WILL THERE BE A MORNING
        LIKE THE MORNING IN THOSE EYES?

BARRY: WHEN THE LONG NIGHT OF GRIEVING IS DONE,

HAROLD: WHEN THE DEAD ARE RELEASED,

BARRY: WHEN THE SHADOWS GIVE WAY TO THE SUN,
HAROLD: TURN YOUR EYES TO THE EAST.
HAROLD/BARRY: SEE THE STAR THAT IS GLOWING, AND IT GLOWS AS
           A SIGN
           THAT THE LIGHT OF THE MORNING SOON WILL SHINE;
           SEE THE EYES OF THE LIVING, AND AT LAST REALISE
           THERE HAS ALWAYS BEEN MORNING,
           THERE HAS ALWAYS BEEN MORNING,
           THERE WILL ALWAYS BE MORNING IN THEIR EYES.

They shake hands and part. CLARRIE *and* JOY *pass.*

CLARRIE: JOYCIE SLOCUM…
JOY: CLARRIE NUGENT…
CLARRIE: JOYCIE NUGENT…

They see MICK *approaching.*

MICK: Peg? Peggy? Oh. Just looking for… Have you seen her?
CLARRIE: Sorry, mate.

MICK *goes.*

   Poor beggar. Come on, I'll see you home.
JOY: I might take a walk by the water. Clear my head for the morning.
CLARRIE: Oh. Right you are.

He kisses her. She watches him go.

JOY: JOYCIE SLOCUM… JOYCIE NUGENT…

She goes as CATHY *pursues* HAROLD.

HAROLD: I can't do it, Cathy.
CATHY: It's me that's doing it. But I need your help.
HAROLD: Do you know where you're heading?
CATHY: Did you know when you were my age?
HAROLD: I had no choice. I was working.

They discover RUBY.

RUBY: You want to run away?
CATHY: I wasn't talking to you.
RUBY: Why leave Turna when things are looking up?
CATHY: I don't belong here.

RUBY: Of course you do!

CATHY: No. I never have. If I belong anywhere, it's somewhere else.

RUBY: Not in a tent show. It's a God-awful life.

HAROLD: Steady on. If she's set on going, we can't stop her. But if you go, Cathy, you go alone. We can't take you in.

CATHY: But I'm not aiming to be a showie. I just want to go with you.

RUBY: You travel with us, kiddo, you're one of us.

CATHY: Might be what I'm meant to be.

RUBY: We can't let you do this to yourself, Cathy.

CATHY: You'll go and tell Dad!

HAROLD: We certainly won't. What you do with your own life is your own affair, but Ruby's right. We can't help you get away.

CATHY: You bugger! You started all this.

HAROLD: Perhaps I did. But I never meant to. You go off and have a good long think, no, a good long sleep. And tomorrow morning things will look very different.

> *He steers her off into the night.*

That was nice, Rube. Felt like we were a bit of a team again.

RUBY: Felt like we were her mum and dad. And that's half true, isn't it? [*Beat.*] Exactly half.

HAROLD: You're sharp, Ruby.

RUBY: Well, they're not Nancy's eyes she's got. You took in every word that kid said. You listened and answered. Long time since I've seen you do that. Are you listening now? You better be. I just steered Renie off towards Barry Doyle. Make the best of what you've got, I said to her. But that won't work for me. What I've got is nothing. Funny, I'm a sharp Sydney girl, but I had to come to a one-horse town to learn to see straight. And I don't see us going forward, Harold. We're not a team. You're not here with me, and I can't see how you ever will be.

HAROLD: Look again.

RUBY: Oh, Christ, you're not crying? That's dirty.

> HAROLD *kneels.*

HAROLD: Forgive me. I've been a mongrel bastard to you. I'm sorry.

RUBY: What does sorry mean, Harold? Sorry till next time?

HAROLD: It means turn me round. I want to go forward. Every word you said to Barry about Renie, I heard it loud and clear. Here and now, darling. There's my New Year's resolution, I'll go for the here and now.

RUBY: Because there's no one better on the horizon?

HAROLD: There is no one better. No one better.

RUBY: Thank you. It's been a big night. I reckon we've earned a nightcap. Come on. Hey… that fella you came back for, did you ever find him?

HAROLD: He's dead, Rube. Dead and gone. But I suppose you twigged that too? So here I am… here we are, starting again with nothing.

RUBY: Not quite nothing, darl.

> *She takes his hand.* MAISIE *comes on as they go. Note: in recent productions, the scene ended here, but in an earlier version, it continued with the following number. A cut may be made from here to the beginning of the final scene.*

MAISIE: SOMETHING ON THE WIND TURNS NOTHING INTO SOMETHING…

> CATHY, PEG *and* JOY *emerge from the darkness.*

CATHY: Is the whole bloody town out here tonight?

JOY: Town and troupe, lovey.

PEG: Why are you out so late?

CATHY: I got all these questions in my head.

JOY: You're not Robinson Crusoe there.

> LORNA, RUBY *and* RENIE *are elsewhere, but watching* PEG, CATHY *and* JOY. *Other* TOWN WOMEN *may join them.*

CATHY: SOMETHING ON THE WIND…

PEG: THE ANSWER ON THE AIR IS…

RENIE: STAY IF YOU HAVE TO, GO IF YOU WANT TO, YES IF YOU'RE READY, NO IF YOU'RE NOT.

CATHY: THE ANSWER ON THE AIR IS…

RUBY: SOMETHING BEHIND YOU,

RUBY/MAISIE: SOMETHING BEFORE YOU…

ALL: THE WORD ON THE WIND IS…

CATHY/JOY/PEG: WHAT?

    THERE IS THE TOWN, THERE IS THE ROAD,

RUBY/RENIE/LORNA/MAISIE: AT THE START OF A YEAR AND THE END OF
          A WEEK,

CATHY: SOMEBODY'S DAUGHTER

PEG: ALONE BY THE WATER,

JOY: FACING THE BRIDGE

ALL: THAT CROSSES THE CREEK.
        AND THE AIR IS SWEET AND COOL, AND MURMURS ITS
        ANSWER—

CATHY: TELL ME THE ANSWER,

JOY/PEG: OFFER SOME CLUES.

ALL: AND THE ANSWER ON THE AIR I HEAR IN THE DARKNESS,
        CLEAR IN THE DARKNESS, THE WORD ON THE WIND IS:
        CHOOSE.

JOY/RUBY: ALL THE YEARS ON THE ROAD,

LORNA/RENIE: ALL THE YEARS IN THIS TOWN,

MAISIE: IF THE AIR BREATHED ITS WISDOM,

CATHY/JOY/PEG: THEN I MISSED WHAT IT SAID.

RUBY/RENIE/LORNA/MAISIE: BUT TONIGHT BY THE WATER

CATHY/JOY/PEG/MAISIE: SOMEBODY'S DAUGHTER

ALL: LOOKS TO THE NIGHT AND THE AIR OVERHEAD.

PEG: AND I'M LOOKING TO THE AIR TO GIVE ME THE ANSWER,
        TELL ME THE ANSWER, WHERE SHOULD I BE?

MAISIE: AND THE ANSWER ON THE AIR

RENIE/LORNA/MAISIE: IS FIND WHAT YOU'RE WANTING,

LORNA/MAISIE/RENIE/RUBY: SEEK WHAT YOU'RE NEEDING,

PEG: THE WORD ON THE WIND IS…

    PEG *goes.*

CATHY/JOY: AND I'M LOOKING TO THE AIR TO GIVE ME AN ANSWER,
        TELL ME THE ANSWER, WHERE SHOULD I BE?

RUBY/RENIE/LORNA/MAISIE: AND THE ANSWER ON THE AIR WILL SPEAK
        IN THE SILENCE…

CATHY/JOY: THE WORD ON THE WIND IS: FREE, FREE…

    JOY *goes.*

CATHY: FREE.

    She runs off. MAISIE *sees her go.*

SCENE SIX

Outside the Shamrock, New Year's Day. A bright, hot morning. JOHNNY *brings bags.* JOY *appears.*

JOY: You seen Dad?

JOHNNY: They're not out of bed yet.

> CLARRIE *appears in the street.*

You mean you haven't told him yet?

CLARRIE: Time and a place for everything, son.

JOHNNY: Reckon.

> *He takes the bags to the truck.*

CLARRIE: First thing this morning, Joycie, what do you know? The wireless starts working again, just like that. I said you were my lucky charm.

JOY: We'll see about that when I've found Dad.

> *She goes indoors as* BARRY *and* RENIE *come from the store.* BARRY *is still wearing last night's clothes. He kisses her and goes into the pub. She sees* CLARRIE.

CLARRIE: Morning, Reen.

RENIE: Morning, Clarrie. Glorious day, isn't it? Good to see the sun again, of course I'll be all day mopping the mud off my floors, mind you, this time next week we'll be moaning about the dust, never satisfied, us human beings.

CLARRIE: Oh, I don't know about that, Reen.

> *She goes.* HAROLD *appears, smartly dressed.* JOY *follows him.*

JOY: Dad, I've got something to tell you.

HAROLD: Later, Joycie. We've got a truck to pack. Come on.

> HAROLD *goes.* RUBY *comes out with her bags.*

RUBY: Christ, is this what it's like?

JOY: What?

RUBY: Early morning. Where's your bag, darl? [*She glances at* CLARRIE.] Or shouldn't I ask?

JOY *helps her to the truck as* PEG *comes out with her broom.* RED *and* LORNA *approach with parcels.*

RED: We haven't missed them, have we?

PEG: They're packing the truck.

LORNA *glances at* PEG, *then gives a parcel to* RED.

LORNA: Take these, Red. I'll be there in a sec.

He goes. PEG *sweeps.*

Peggy, what's up?

PEG: If you're asking, you don't need an answer.

LORNA: But it's... Peg, put the broom down! It's over, isn't it?

JOHNNY *appears from the truck. They see him.*

I didn't have a clue, not till I saw you dancing with him. That dress had a life of its own. But that was one night. Rum punch and dancing and moonlight. I remember the night you got engaged...

PEG: Please, Lorna...

LORNA: You wore pale pink, with a deep rose sash. And there was Mick with his hair slicked down and his suit smelling of Murlex, trying to get through the Pride of Erin. He was never a dancer, was he? But he'd always have a go.

JOHNNY *reaches them.*

Morning, Johnny. Safe journey.

She hurries off to the truck.

JOHNNY: I bet you didn't sleep a wink. I didn't.

PEG: Mick never come in last night. I hope to God he's all right.

JOHNNY: Don't you reckon that's a sign? He means to let you slip away?

MAISIE *arrives with parcels.*

MAISIE: Peggy. Glorious morning. John, where are the rest of the travellers? Here. Scones, pikelets, rock cakes...

JOHNNY: Thanks. If you'd put them in the truck for us...

She glances at both of them.

MAISIE: Of course.

She goes to the truck.

JOHNNY: Today or never. We both know that, don't we? Today or never.

They see MICK *approaching.*

If it's today, climb in the back of the truck.

He goes.

PEG: Where were you?

MICK: Out looking for you. Then I reckoned you probably didn't want to be found. I slept beside the creek. First time in months I got to sleep sober. I've been a streak of misery, haven't I? Never noticing a bloody thing. Last night I saw you dancing in that dress... A blind man, that's me. One crook leg, two bung eyes. And one heart, thumping away in here. I don't have the words to say what's inside me. Only I want to start again. If it's not too late. Peggy, if you want to go, go quick. If you're going to stay... well, it shouldn't be pity keeping you here.

All return from the truck. The whole TOWN *is present.*

MAISIE: Ladies and gentlemen, Harold, I have a presentation—

CLARRIE: Hang on, Maise.

MAISIE: After you, Clarence.

CLARRIE: We got an announcement to make. Joycie?

JOY: Dad, I'm not coming with you. I'm staying here with Clarrie.

HAROLD: You can't do this to me!

BARRY: Let her go, mate.

HAROLD: But I've given this girl everything.

JOY: And I've given it back with interest. Now I need to settle down.

HAROLD: Settle down? You wouldn't know how.

RUBY: She's got plenty of time to learn.

JOY: Think of me as your gift to Turnaround Creek.

RENIE: It'd be a lovely gesture, Harold.

HAROLD: [*to* JOY] Joycie... you're my gift to Turnaround Creek.

CLARRIE: Whacko!

MAISIE: You haven't had Turnaround Creek's gift to you! The key to the School of Arts.

She hangs it around HAROLD's *neck.*

HAROLD: Thank you.

MAISIE: Thank you.

RUBY: No, thank you. You've given us so much.

BARRY: You've given us... I'm no speech-maker. You've given us—

CLARRIE: Joy.

BARRY: Yes. And a chance to look at ourselves. Harold?

HAROLD: Christmas Eve, how long ago was that? Nine days. We had nothing. We came here. Nine days on, and what do we have? A key to the hall, food for the road, petrol, a truck in working order, thanks to Mick, but... something else. What?

CLARRIE: Crikey. I know what. Harold. Rainbow Gal. Came in yesterday at fifty-to-one. Two hundred and fifty smackers to get you on your way.

He hands over a wad of notes.

BARRY: Look at Harold. He's speechless.

RUBY: The show's over. Come on.

The TROUPE *head for the truck.*

JOHNNY/MICK: I MET THE WOMAN UNDERNEATH THE CASUARINA TREE,

PEG: I HEARD THE DISTANT THUNDER, NOW THE CREEK IS RUNNING FREE,

PEG/JOHNNY: I SAW THE NINE-DAY WONDER, AND AS IT MOVES AWAY,

JOHNNY: IT SAYS TODAY OR NEVER...

PEG: NEVER...

ALL: NEW YEAR HERE, A NINE-DAY WONDER GONE...

MICK: THE ONLY SIGN OF CHRISTMAS WAS THE SHE-OAK IN THE BAR,

LORNA: WITH COTTON-WOOL FOR SNOWBALLS, AND A SILVER PAPER STAR,

RED: UNTIL WE FELT THE BREEZE COME UP AND STIR THE WEATHERVANE,

BARRY: AND THEN WE SAW THE WONDER, THE COMING OF THE RAIN.

TOWN: AND AS THE RAIN KEPT COMING, THE OLD YEAR PASSED AWAY,

TROUPE: AND AS WE TAKE THE ROAD AGAIN, A NEW YEAR STARTS TODAY;

ALL: WHEN NOTHING TURNS TO SOMETHING, WHAT WILL TOMORROW BRING?

TODAY A NINE-DAY WONDER, TOMORROW, ANYTHING.

MOUTHS WERE WIDE WITH WONDER, DRANK THE SUMMER RAIN,

LAST WEEK OUR HOPE WAS DYING, TODAY IT LIVES AGAIN,

FOR NOTHING TURNED TO SOMETHING, ALTHOUGH WE DON'T KNOW HOW;

THERE GOES A NINE-DAY WONDER, I WONDER WHAT COMES NOW?

NEW YEAR HERE, A NINE-DAY WONDER GONE...

The TROUPE *drive away. The* TOWN *go inside.* PEG *sweeps.* MICK *whittles.* BARRY *comes out of the pub.*

BARRY: Cathy's gone.

They look towards the vanishing truck.

CURTAIN

www.ingramcontent.com/pod-product-compliance
Lightning Source LLC
Chambersburg PA
CBHW041931090426
42744CB00017B/2017